Keep Paddling Against the Wind

Aatak Ayguumun Angwaaghnaqi

Yaari Walker

Copyright © 2024
All Rights Reserved

All rights reserved. No part of this memoir may be reproduced, distributed, or transmitted in any form or by any means, including photocopying, recording, or other electronic or mechanical methods, without the prior written permission of the author, except in the case of brief quotations embodied in critical reviews and certain other noncommercial uses permitted by copyright law

This book is for the homeless man that stands at the intersection, the individual who survived abuse, the one who abused who is hurting too, the child who witnessed abuse, the people who work at the clinics and hospitals, the police officers and investigators, the teachers and professors, the counselors and clinicians, the students from high school on up, the people who work at homeless shelters and in treatment centers, the people who are receiving inpatient and outpatient treatment, for the ones who are in anger management, this book is for people who need to understand there are communication and cultural differences.

This book is for the homeless man that stands at the intersection, the individual who survived abuse, the one who abused who is hurting too, the child who witnessed abuse, the people who work at the clinics and hospitals, the police officers and investigators, the teachers and professors, the counselors and clinicians, the students from high school on up, the people who work at homeless shelters and in treatment centers, the people who are receiving inpatient and outpatient treatment, for the ones who are in anger management, this book is for people who need to understand there are communication and cultural differences.

Table of Contents

Chapter One 1
   As I Became Aware 1

Chapter Two 6
   Generational Trauma 6
   Trauma, Colonization, and Assimilation 7

Chapter Three 12
   Fourteen-Years-Old 12

Chapter Four 14
   Shamanism: AKA Traditional Healing 14

Chapter Five 16
   Alaska Native Languages and Communication Styles ... 16

Chapter Six 18
   In Love and a Suicide Attempt 18

Chapter Seven 21
   The Next Step 21

Chapter Eight 24
   In Love Again 24

Chapter Nine 32
   An Angel Saved Me 32

Chapter Ten 34
   My Mother Apologizes to my Siblings and I 34

Chapter Eleven 36
   Can I brave leaving now? 36

Chapter Twelve 39
   Moving Again 39

Chapter Thirteen	46
I Need Help	46
Chapter Fourteen	51
My New Boyfriend	51
Chapter Fifteen	64
Spirituality	64
Chapter Sixteen	82
The Last Time	82
Chapter Seventeen	87
Healing Center	87
Chapter Eighteen	90
Triggers	90
Chapter Nineteen	91
I'm a Survivor	91
Conclusion	**93**
For My Mother	95
Acknowledgements	97
About the Author	i

Chapter One

As I Became Aware

As I became aware, I would fall asleep on my apa's (sounds like up-ah - grandfather) shoulders with my cheek resting on his head as he walked. It was so comfortable for me because I felt so safe with him. As I became aware, my apa would have me sitting on his lap while having tea. I remember hearing stories told by him and others in our language. I really miss that so much! As I grew older, I would be sitting on my apa's lap while he was drumming and singing. No matter how loud the drummers and singers were, I managed to fall asleep to the beat of the drum. I would sleep between my grandparents until I turned seven or eight. I felt so loved by them. Even after the age of eight, my nengyuq (sounds like nung-yook – grandmother) would bathe me in front of the heater so I don't get cold. She would dress me warm in the wintertime with handmade atkuk (winter parka) that she stitched together by hand.

Our grandparents helped raise my siblings, me, and other grandchildren. It's the norm in our culture for grandchildren to be raised, especially by our paternal grandparents, because of our clan protocols. At that time, my parents and us children lived at my grandparents' house because of the lack of housing in the village. With our clan system in place, we are part of our father's clan and a patrilineal society. In some cases, a mother's child would be raised by her parents too. That's just the way it is. My siblings and I were very fortunate to have also been raised by our paternal grandparents.

My apa used to call me "Mom" because I was named after his mother, Yaari, who passed on her name to me three months before I was born while she was on her deathbed. She came from a different clan, so she permitted my clan people for me to carry on her name. They say in our culture that those who are named after loved ones gone before us carry on characteristics of the individual they are named after. Relatives who knew her have told me in the past that I was just like my great-grandmother Yaari. I received confirmation one day when she came to me while I was in my sacred space and told me that I was just like her. I always used to wonder about her. I now know I have some of her characteristics. I carry her with me.

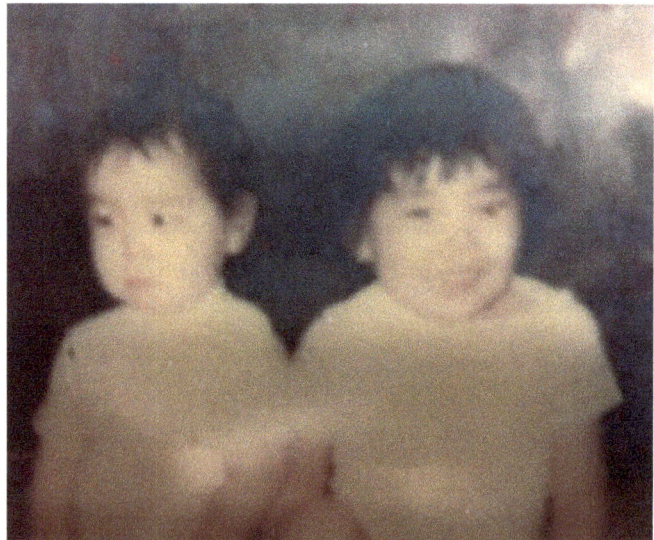

I remember as a little girl while we were at Northeast Cape on St. Lawrence Island, my apa held my hand as we walked through the old houses. He pointed through a broken window at a homemade baby crib and told me it once belonged to me. When I think back to moments as a little girl with my paternal grandparents, it was one of the best days of my life. I felt safe, loved, well taken care of, and so much positive energy from both of them. If my siblings and I made bad choices, our grandmother would sit us down and teach us Yupik values, which are words to live by. She was the Yupik disciplinarian. I am very glad she did that because when you hear the same things over and over, they are easier to remember. Sometimes, I do forget because it's human nature. I have to shift myself when I am reminded.

Our grandmother was very Yupik strict. She constantly reminded us children how not to behave. These were ancient teachings passed down through generations that we call Yupik traditional values. I remember one night, my cousin and I were having so much fun when I was twelve years old! We kept whispering in each other's ears and laughing. I don't think we were making fun of anyone, just enjoying each other. When I got home that night, my grandmother sat me down and said, "I'm glad you and your cousin were having so much fun at atuq (Eskimo dance), but what you girls were doing was not okay. It is not okay to whisper in someone else's ear in the presence of others and laugh out loud because someone might think you girls were making fun of them.." It was a respect thing.

As I was growing up, I remember I used to play at the beach with my friends. We used rocks to play house, and we pretended we had two parents and children. There were times I played mom and sometimes a daughter. We would take mud and pretend we were baking chocolate cake or cupcakes. We used small pieces of sticks and rocks to create furniture. I remember how fun it was to be an architect and home decorator. Those are some of my best memories of my childhood days with my friends. I miss those days. I felt so safe with my grandparents.

There was a playground outside the school where there were slides, swings, and an outdoor basketball court. We played Helicopter over my head, jump rope, and tag on the basketball court. These were the days I was starting to explore smoking cigarettes, huffing gasoline, and asphyxiation. I was twelve years old when I started to experiment with my friends. What happened to me at twelve?

I remember in middle school, one or two of us would have these bandanas that we took with us to school. We also took turns stealing cigarettes from our parents and brought them with us to school. We would also take plastic bags, put toilet paper in them, and pour gasoline in the bag so we could huff. Occasionally, one of us would steal shoe goop from the Native store to use for huffing. We did all these things during our lunch break, right after school, and sometimes in the evenings until it was time for us to go home for curfew. Then, I started to experiment with marijuana. I discovered that I really liked it because it made me laugh literally at nothing. Every time I smoked marijuana, I would just laugh, and laugh, and laugh. When I was done laughing, I would just sit there and space out. I smoked marijuana sometimes during lunch break, after school, and in the evenings. How did I live through all of this? I could have died hundreds of times over.

Many bad things happened when I was at the age of twelve. I remember one summer, the City of Savoonga hosted an event for a village-wide clean-up. The person who picked the most trash bags of garbage would win a bicycle. I wanted to win that bike so badly that I worked hard. A relative of mine told me there was lots of trash behind one of the teacher housings, where literally no one goes. I believed him. He cornered me, tried to kiss me on my neck and held me tight. He tried to pull my pants down, but I fought really hard. He was much stronger than me. He managed to pull my pants part way down. Survival mode kicked in inside me, and I managed to escape. He chased me, but I outran him. I remember how terrified I was. I never told anyone because I was worried no one would believe me.

In the same year, we went to fish camp and a family "friend" came with us. My parents loved him! They trusted him. He did a lot of things for our family that earned my parents' trust. One night, I woke up in the middle of the night. I found myself in his sleeping bag with my panty off. I remember thinking of how I ended up in his sleeping bag. I was scared to tell my parents what happened. I was scared they would not believe me, so I never told them. It took me 30 years to start talking about it a little bit at 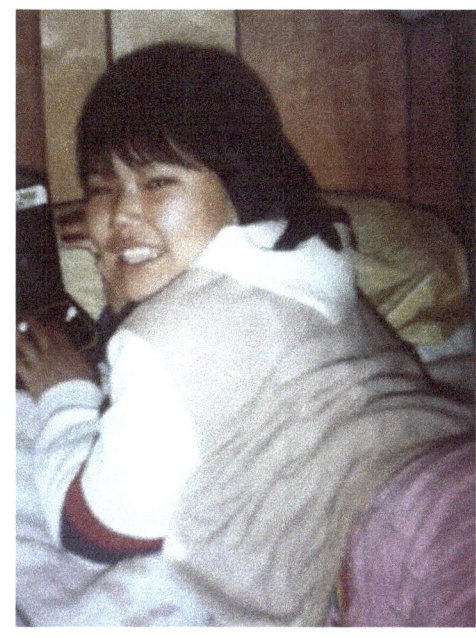 a time. It was hard for me to talk about it. This was the start of the twelve-year-old girl trapped inside me for a few decades. I carried her inside me, and she felt broken.

When I lived with my grandparents, I learned a lot. My grandmother taught us a lot about behavior: piniiqelleq atuqluku – use love, Ilaasi kayusitaqluki – help others, Ilaasi tuunaqluki – share with others, atunem ilaasi – treat everyone with the same respect, esghaghsaqegpenang – don't try to get attention (it means don't be loud, don't be proud, and don't dress revealing), sivulighaayugtegpenang – don't try to be first at anything, sigutqumsugpenang – don't whisper in other peoples ears in front of others, uguumikeraaghpenang – don't be a bully, siivanlleghet nagaataqluki – listen to the Elders, angaayuqaasi nagaataqluki – listen to your parents, yughaaghaqlusi – always pray, ilaasi esghaapagtekefqiita – don't let your friends watch you eat or drink, offer them, yiilgigpenasi – don't talk about others behind their backs, tawaaten aneghtegpenang – don't breathe like that, seghleghyugsaghpenang – don't try to make others feel bad about themselves. These are just some of the teachings that shape us into who we are as Yupik people.

My apa had more of a leadership role in the community, so he instilled those in us while we were growing up. He reminded us never to talk about "karma" because it is not up to man, it is up to nature. He taught us to live our lives to not judge others because it is not our job. When you are a leader, you lead with love, kindness, and respect. You never shame the people you are leading and never correct them in front of others. You avoid yelling at them. When you lead them as a "boss", people give you less respect. There is a difference between a boss and a leader. People will be more drawn to you if you lead with respect. You listen to the people, and you pay attention to their needs. It is not about you or your ego; it is about the people you are serving. When you are a leader, you are a serviceman or woman. In what way are you being of service to your community? As my apa would say, "Piniitungwaaq igleghutinaqelghaaten – try your best to be a good leader". I serve people and I love doing it the best way I know how. I am not perfect and I make mistakes, but I learn as I go. We get better and stronger as we experience life.

Chapter Two

Generational Trauma

By the time I was twelve, we had moved into a new four-bedroom house on the south side of the village. It felt kind of weird to me because I was so used to most of the houses being towards the beach which is on the north side of the village. I remember how happy I was to have my very own bedroom! I really enjoyed decorating my bedroom. That was the first time I realized I enjoyed home decorating. After we moved into the house, things started to change. I have memories of my mother as a pre-teen, who I felt like she was just physically there. My mother was not present for us children. She was never an emotional support, and she just didn't know how. It was one of my darkest times. My mother became abusive to my siblings and me after we moved into our new home, especially to the middle child – my sister. I have memories of my mother grabbing my sister by the hair, dragging her down the hallway and yelling at her. She beat her in front of my brother and I. She would take a broomstick and beat me on my legs. I have memories of the pain. I never knew what child abuse was until we moved into our new home. We never told our father she abused us, and she never did it in front of our father. I remember one time she used the broomstick on me at her parents' house in front of them. My grandfather stopped her, "Aghyughpenaan tawaaten – don't use physical punishment." My mother was mean, especially when she drank alcohol. I used to be scared of her when she would drink alcohol. This all happened when we moved to Anchorage for a year or two. I remember trying to hide my sister and protect her under a table or blanket. As small as I was, I would hold my sister and try to protect her from my mom. I think I was about five years old my first memory trying to protect my sister. I never wanted to be around her, especially when she was under the influence of alcohol. I was very scared of my mom when my dad wasn't around. I felt so powerless and helpless. Who is this woman?

Trauma, Colonization, and Assimilation

First, the Yankee whalers almost decimated the animals our ancestors survived off of for many generations, then many of our people died of famine, starvation, and diseases, then the church arrived, and the boarding school era began. Since the first explorers arrived, our Alaska Native people have been told how to live. Many of our rights were taken away by force. Alaska Native people became one of the most regulated people in the United States. The federal government issued these blood quantum cards to Alaska Native and Native American people in the United States. With these blood quantum cards in place, it determined if you were eligible for certain services. To me, it feels like these cards were also issued to make Alaska Native people disappear. If you fall below a certain blood quantum, you are not Native enough to receive these services. So, according to these blood quantum cards, you are not Native enough. No matter what these federal government-issued cards determine, you are Native. Whether you have a drop of blood or more, you are Native. The government does not get to decide who is Native and who is not. You carry the genes of your ancestors. Your DNA carries knowledge that you may never realize you had. Some of our cultural ways were passed down through generations without realizing some of these traditions came from our ancestors. For instance, making dry fish is a part of some of our Native cultures. It has been the norm in our families that we may not have realized it was part of our culture. The government – it's not for all people, but for some. We are not some of those people on their agenda. That is what makes me feel like we are still invisible today. We need our own lawmakers, policymakers, researchers, and educators. Or at least have our own Indigenous people help integrate these into place. This entire system was made by one culture only. They say Anchorage is the most diverse city in the United States. If that is the case, why is the entire system based only on one culture? Why can't we integrate our Alaska Native ways into education, policies, etc.? Why can't we integrate American-Japanese ways into this system? The Samoan, Mexican, and Native American ways? Imagine how much stronger our society would be if we took our Alaska Native values and included them in laws and policies.

In 1881, Sheldon Jackson was appointed by the federal government to come to Alaska to introduce Alaska Native people to Western education and religion. The intention of the government was to assimilate and colonize Alaska Native people. The government wanted to erase our Alaska Native cultures. They did everything in their power to take away our cultures and traditions, but here we still stand, and our cultures are thriving. Our Alaska Native traditions are coming back to life little by little. Some Alaska Native Elders share their memories about their cultures that help us to bring back the old ways. Some come from books and stories passed down through generations. We use pictures and old videos to bring our cultures back to life. In some villages, their traditions thrived; in some villages, they lost a lot of the ancient traditions that once kept their people healthy and thriving.

When the missionaries arrived in the late 1800's, they were sent to the villages in Rural Alaska. Some children were forcefully taken away, and some parents willingly let their children go because they trusted the church. Religion and spirituality have some similarities, and that is why parents trusted the church. Some children as young as five years old were sent as far away as Carlisle, Pennsylvania, which was one of the worst boarding schools in the history of the United States. Children were all forms of abuse by the missionary schools. No child was allowed to speak their mother tongue, to wear their traditional clothing, to have long hair, or to practice our cultures and traditions. The hands of the schools and the Church emotionally, mentally, physically, spiritually, and sexually abused children. Some young girls were sent back to their villages impregnated. Some children never made it back to their homes to their families, killed by the hands of the schools and the Church. Some children were buried underground with no names on their headstones. I cannot imagine how traumatized these children were while they were in boarding schools. It is painful just to think about it. Imagine your child being forcefully taken away from your care and sent far away from home, and you do not know how they are doing, when they will return, or if they will return. Imagine the school officials and the Churches making their parents believe they are in good hands but were abused.

Native children were not allowed to comfort each other. They were not allowed to hold each other or lift each other up. If a child was caught trying to comfort another child, they would be physically punished. If a child was caught speaking in their mother tongue, they would be beaten and/or hand soap put in their mouths. Imagine a Native adult doing that to your child, forcing you to speak their Indigenous language. You were not allowed to speak English.

This form of abuse went on for many decades among the Alaska Native people. In my family, my parents' generation were the last ones to endure abuse while in boarding school. My father was sent to Wrangell Institute in Southeast Alaska, which was one of the worst boarding schools in the United States. My mother went to a boarding school in Oregon. I do not know how my parents were treated while in boarding school, and I do not want to know. I asked my father once, but he told me he was treated okay. I was too scared to ask him anything else. I'm too scared to ask my mother. I learned that even if some children were not abused in school, they experienced a loss of identity of their Alaska Native cultures. They were not allowed to be an Indigenous person. As a result of these boarding schools, thousands of our Alaska Native people do not know how to speak their languages. Language is so important because it teaches us how to be. There are no words in the English language to describe some of our words that teach us how to live our lives, such as "aneghneq" – it translates into breath, but it is not just a form of breathing; it is a way of life. Our Elders teach us to use breathe in a good way. You know the saying "Don't waste your breath"? It is something along the lines of that, but it has a deeper meaning.

When the children left school and became parents, many refused to teach their children their languages. Some parents reported that their Native language was beaten out of them and that they forgot how to speak their languages. When some boarding school survivors became parents, they did not know how to parent their children. Generational and inter-generational trauma became a big issue among Alaska Native people. As a result of the missionaries and the boarding schools, Alaska Native people today have the highest rates of suicide, domestic violence, child abuse, sexual abuse, alcoholism, homelessness, children in foster care, and the highest incarceration by percentage. When is the government going to hold themselves accountable? I used to be a very angry person because of the history of boarding schools and the church. We all need healing from the past, and so do our oppressors. Our ancestors need healing too. I'm happy to see more and more healing activities and events happening in our community. Our cultures and traditions are thriving and coming back to life. Our qayaqs (kayaks) are making a strong comeback, our taatuuqs (tattoos) are alive once again, one poke and stitch at a time, and our mask rituals are waking up! Our spirits and our DNA remember who we are as Native people.

I used to think that healing would not happen for us until the government came forward to own up to the trauma inflicted on us Alaska Natives. I've changed my mindset and decided healing is up to us. We may never see the government come forward and apologize to the Alaska Native people. It is time for us to surrender and move towards forgiveness and healing. Healing is up to you and me. Nothing or no one will take what we have from us again. Alaska Native peoples' voices are powerful, strong, and are now starting to be heard today. We still have some work to do. We still fight for our rights, but things are slowly changing. In 2024, we are still the most regulated people in the United States. We are still fighting for our rights. They once tried to erase who we are, but because they can't do that, they try to limit our access to the resources that help us to survive. We will stay stood.

When the denominations arrived in the villages, they banned a lot of the ancient practices of the Alaska Native people. In some villages, singing and dancing were banned, making our Indigenous people believe that it was a sin. Today, some of our Alaska Native people believe it because of what the church taught them. It is a way of celebration, storytelling, preserving history, entertainment, for good health, and some songs are prayer songs. Our hand and arm motions tell stories of the songs. Motions were kind of like sign language, and they have meaning. Traditionally, when we danced, we stood stationary in one spot because when we danced in a small room, there wasn't a lot of room to move our feet around. At least, that is what I was taught. Women bounce at their knees, and men stomp one foot to the beat of the drum. In other Alaska Native cultures, such as in Southwest Alaska, men kneel in front of the women. It is a respectful thing. Women being the main dancers, men kneeled out of respect so the audience can see the women dance. In Southeast Alaska there are more foot movement and their styles of drums are different than the Eskimo groups, they use handheld drums. Regardless of what part of Alaska you came from, our traditions of songs and dances had some similarities in terms of our cultures, stories, and beliefs.

Chapter Three

Fourteen-Years-Old

At the age of fourteen, in the ninth grade, I started to question my existence. I was going through an identity crisis. Who am I? Why am I here? Are my parents my real parents? Was I adopted? I couldn't answer these questions, but I started to think very deeply about my purpose in life. I suddenly decided I would no longer hang out with my friends, who have been my friends since childhood. I quit smoking cigarettes and marijuana, quit huffing shoe goop and gasoline, and quit asphyxiating. I put behind me what the two men did to me. I was trying so hard to find who I was. I became very serious about life and school. I started doing better in school and never hung out with my friends anymore, not because I didn't want to, but because I was just trying to discover who I was. My parents asked me if I was okay because they saw the changes in me. They were worried that I no longer wanted to be with my friends, and it worried them. At the end of my freshman year in high school, I was named the student of the year. I had perfect attendance and a high honor roll. I received a certificate from the school "Student of the Year" (1983-84).

After I was named the student of the year, I started to get bullied by older girls. I remember how hard I tried to show no emotions because I didn't want them to see me cry. Some girls would spit in my face, pull the shower curtain in the girls' shower room at the gym, call me names, and show so much hate towards me. Some girls would throw their homework at me, "Do my homework, you smart b****." I would just sit there in silence and just stare at the floor. I tried so hard to be strong on the outside, but it was tearing me up on the inside. Some of the girls didn't want me on the girls' basketball team, but I joined anyway. The more they bullied me, the harder I worked at basketball and in school. I wanted to prove to them that I was good enough. I chose not to respond to them as if they were not there. I felt like I had no friends. I was bullied into my sophomore year. I never told my parents or anyone that at least 4-5 girls were bullying me. One day, I finally cried to my mother but wouldn't tell her what was happening. I finally told her, but she reacted out of anger. It was not okay by the way she reacted towards that girl.

Chapter Four

Shamanism: AKA Traditional Healing

What once kept our ancestors healthy, the church banned from our villages. We had our own doctors, counselors, guides, wisdom keepers, and seers today known as shamans. The word shaman comes from a reindeer herding group of people from Siberia. The word was traditionally "Saman", the ones who know. In our language, we call them "Alignalghii" or "Aglignalghii". In other Alaska Native languages, they are called different things.

The shamans' work was very important and they were highly respected in the native communities. They practiced spirituality for their healing work for the people. When the shamans worked with individuals in the community, they knew exactly what the individuals needed because they could see, feel, and hear what the naked eye could not. It was almost as if they had x-ray eyes. Their spirit helpers or Creator would reveal what the individual needs were. They made medicines from different types of plants that they gathered from nature that they used for themselves and community members. Each healing session with people was never the same because everyone had different needs. My ancestors, spirit helpers, or Creator revealed some techniques.

When I was twelve years old, one of my uncles told me if our people were still practicing shamanism that, I would have been one. I never understood what it meant or what it was, because I never heard about "Shamans" in my life before. Later in my teen years, I began to understand what he was talking about. I learned about our ancient healing methods in my high school years through some stories by my grandfather. I heard stories of how shamans were able to shape-shift into other forms of beings and how they would fly and run at a very fast speed. I heard they could heal people and that they were our wisdom keepers. I didn't learn much about them until later on in life. By the time I was nineteen years old, something urged me to tell my grandmother about my hot hands. My grandmother said, "Iiggeten maatneghqwaanghata kina saafluku yughaatkaqluku". In my mind, I said I wouldn't do that because people would think I was crazy. What she said was, "When your hands get hot, I want you to touch someone and I want you to pray for them.". I never quite fully understood what that meant. Growing up I experienced things I never heard people talk about. I kept them to myself because I was worried people would think I was crazy. I used to wonder if I was alone. Why didn't I hear people talk about these things if I wasn't alone? I wondered, "Are these normal?". I saw, heard, sensed, and felt the unseen but never talked about them because of my fear of being called crazy, judged, or not believed.

Chapter Five

Alaska Native Languages and Communication Styles

Working for the Alaska Native Heritage Center for sixteen years taught me many things about our Alaska Native languages. Language is a form of communication, but it is also a way of life. It teaches us how to behave and how to live our lives as human beings. It teaches us how to communicate with animals and nature, not just people. We also communicate with our spirits when we connect with all things alive, and everything is alive, so language is also a form of spirituality.

In our Alaska Native languages, we have one words that make up whole sentences. The English language seems generalized to me. Some will disagree, and that's okay. For example, "How are you?" – specifically asking one person how they are doing. In my language, "Natetaqsin?" – refers to asking one person how they are doing, and we mean it when we ask. In Western culture, those who find silence to be awkward use it as a filler; it's a ritual. So basically, they say, "I don't really want to know how you are doing, but how are you?". "Natetaqestek" refers to asking two people how they are doing. "Natetaqetsi" – refers to asking three or more people how they are doing? If you especially ask an Alaska Native Elder, "How are you?" I hope you have time because they may just tell you everything about themselves, and you will wonder why they are telling you everything about themselves; that is if you come from a culture who uses "how are you" as a ritual to fill a void.

English being my second language, I used to be terrified of speaking it especially when I traveled outside of my village. I actually used to wish I were a "White person" when I was in middle school. I used to wish my hair was blonde, my eyes were blue, and my skin was fair. I used to be ashamed of being an Alaska Native, and I didn't even realize I felt that way until in my early 20s. I used to feel like Alaska Native people were the minorities of the minorities. I wanted to be outgoing, not afraid to speak English, I used to wish to be smart like a white person. I didn't want people to judge me for my skin color or how I spoke English. I was so ashamed of being dark-skinned. I felt invisible, and I still do to a certain degree today. I feel like Alaska Native people have to work extra hard to be heard, seen, and to have our rights. So many injustices in this day and age in 2024.

It was when I started to work for the Alaska Native Heritage Center that I finally did not feel ashamed to be an Alaska Native. I felt so proud of who I was and where I came from. I realized how our Alaska Native people are so smart for their ingenuity, creativity, resilience, and being able to stand up against the wrong put upon us. It made me feel so proud to be an Alaska Native. This was the start of my healing journey. I felt like some healing energy was starting to move through me once I became proud of who I was and where I came from. I was no longer afraid of being myself. I was no longer afraid to speak up.

Chapter Six

In Love and a Suicide Attempt

In 1984, towards the end of my freshman year in high school, I started dating this boy who was nearly two years older than me. This was after I decided I was done being at home all the time. I was absolutely in love, but shy! It was the absolute best thing that happened to me then! I was just 14 years old, and he was my first love. In my mind, I decided I was going to be with him for the rest of my life! He was so sweet, funny, popular, but mischievous! He was part of this group of boys I thought were pretty cool and popular. I really liked him and his personality. I thought he was handsome! We didn't hang out daily, which made it fun for me. It almost felt like we were just flirting from a distance but not always being together. For some reason, that was fun to me. I thought loud in my head, "I'M SO IN LOVE!"

We dated for a year and a half, and we parted ways. I didn't like how he was starting to get other boys involved in our relationship. It didn't feel right to me. It made me feel disgusted on the inside, but I didn't show it. I just didn't know how to express myself at the time.

I started dating another boy in my sophomore year in high school. He was handsome and popular. My heart fluttered with joy and excitement! I was just head over heels with him and absolutely in love! I truly adored him and I was inseparable from him. We were together daily. I ended up pregnant at the age of sixteen by him. I started to have thoughts of suicide because I was worried my parents would disown me. I didn't want my parents to find out I was pregnant. My father walked in on me as I attempted suicide. He gently took the knife from my hand and held me in his arms while I was sobbing. The heaviness in my heart center area was so heavy, something I never felt before in my life. I couldn't tell him why I attempted suicide, I was too ashamed of myself. I then asked the health aide who told me I was pregnant to wait until I made it to the neighboring village to call my parents to tell them that I was pregnant. When I arrived at Gambell High School for high school basketball, a staff member came to get me, saying I had a phone call. I hesitantly walked to the office to take the call because I knew it was my parents. When I answered the phone, my father asked, "Why didn't you tell us yourself?" I didn't know how to respond, so I just sat there silently crying. My father told me, "We love you no matter what happens and we will always love you." I was in a huge relief when I heard him say those words!

After the ball games in Gambell, we flew back to Savoonga. My parents picked me up from the airport and took me home. My entire family was so loving and kind to me. I asked my sister why everyone was so nice and she said, "Because Dad told us to be nice so you don't hurt yourself." I cried, knowing my family still loved me even if I disappointed my parents. Or were they disappointed in me? I felt like I was not deserving of love. I realized that my parents would always love me no matter what. I really thought they'd disown me and force me to give up my baby. I knew because I was not married to my baby's father that my clan would have power over my baby, meaning my family would make decisions around my baby. My paternal apa was our clan leader, the decision maker and guide at the time.

My father reached out for help for me from Nome Behavior Health. A counselor came to my village. She arrived in a business suit and a name tag. My first impression of her was that she was only there to do her job.

She introduced herself to me and told me her job title, then told me she was going to do an assessment to determine what kind of therapy I needed. I quietly thought in my mind, "Yep. She is only here to do her job. Why should I tell her anything about me?!" My mind was made up that I didn't want to have anything to do with her so I immediately shut down. All I could do was stare at the floor and shrug my shoulders. By shrugging my shoulders, I was sending her messages without even realizing it, "Why should I tell you anything about me? I don't want to speak to you. You don't care about me, you are only here to do your job." she came across to me as a job title, not a caring human being. I didn't find my therapy sessions with her helpful at all. At sixteen, I didn't realize it was because of our cultural differences. How could I trust a stranger to tell my problems if we had zero connections? Had she taken the time to build a relationship with me and get to know me first before any sessions began, I probably would have opened up to her. In our Native communities, relationships are one of the most important things to us. It is a way of connecting with one another for support, help, unity, and community. It goes beyond that, but I think you get the jest of it.

Based on my experience with this counselor, I use it as a tool to educate people about building relationships in the Alaska Native way. This counselor and I when I was suicidal, had no connections and it was a big turn-off for me. I did not want to share my deep secrets and hurts with a complete stranger I knew nothing about. I was not comfortable with her at all. Had she asked me to share who I am and where I come from first before going into her job, I would have opened up to her. Had she told me a little about herself, it would have made me feel more comfortable to share what was deep in my thoughts that no one could get to, not even my parents. I couldn't share my deepest thoughts with just anyone at sixteen. I hid them deep inside me.

Chapter Seven

The Next Step

My parents and I talked about the next steps. We all decided my parents would adopt my baby so I could finish high school and go to college after I graduated. I don't have many memories or feelings throughout my pregnancy other than I was excited for the baby. My mother prepared for the baby throughout my pregnancy gathering needs for the baby. I got so huge that my mom had to clean my feet and help me put my socks and shoes. I was puffy like the Michelin Man! My mother and I had to fly to the hub because there were no hospitals in our village. We flew to Nome three weeks prior to my due date. My dad came to be with us and it meant so much to me that he came. It was a hot summer in Nome! My due date came and gone. When are you going to come, baby?! My baby was ten days over-due. I finally went into labor, and it was very slow. I was in labor for 23.5 hours. I remember I pushed nearly four hours with her. She weighed 8 lbs. 3 oz. and was almost 22 inches long at birth! My parents were so happy to have her. My mother named her after her late mother, Laura. Her great-aunt from her father's side gave her her middle name "Mae Jenane." I really liked how it went well together. My apa named her "Ateka" after his grandmother on his paternal side. So, my baby was named after her great-great grandmother and that was so special!

After my baby was born, I suddenly realized what unconditional love truly meant because that was what I felt for my baby. My parents' first grandchild but they were going to adopt her. I never quite understood the love they had for her yet, but I could see how much they loved her. My parents made sure she had all her needs and made sure she was well taken care of. My sister and I took turns taking care of her too, when our parents weren't home. My sister was spoiling her. She loved being a big sister to a baby girl. I could feel the energy between my sister and baby Laura. I could see and feel how much my sister loved her, making me feel so good inside.

My baby's father came to my village to meet her and to be with us. I really liked watching him hold her and love her up. It meant a lot to me that he came to meet her, although we were not together anymore. I wanted her to know who he was, even if my parents were adopting her. I felt it was important for Laura and her biological father to build a relationship with each other and to know each other.

My parents were very fond of Laura. I could see how much they cared for her and how much they wanted her, and I absolutely loved that. I wouldn't want it any other way and wouldn't want her anywhere else but with my parents. I wanted her to be in our family. My mother especially held her close to her heart. After Laura was born, my mother quit drinking. She wanted to be able to care for Laura in a good way. It made me so happy when she told us she quit drinking for the baby. I hadn't felt this kind of relief. I knew then that baby Laura would be okay.

Chapter Eight

In Love Again

In my junior year in high school, I returned to my first love. We started seeing each other again and we were so in love and happy! We became inseparable. We did everything together in our daily lives. My senior year in high school, I got pregnant with our baby. I was very terrified to tell my parents yet again that I was pregnant for the second time while in high school. I kept it a secret from both my parents and from my boyfriend. I was worried my boyfriend would leave me if I told him I was pregnant. This time, my father was upset when he found out I was pregnant again. We talked about me going to college after high school throughout my high school years. He encouraged me to give my baby up, but in my heart, I knew I couldn't do that, so I decided to keep my baby, but I didn't tell my parents that I had plans to keep him. I wanted my parents to believe I was giving my baby up to some relatives in the village to satisfy them. My heart was so broken that I was expected to give my baby up. It tore me to pieces on the inside. My heart center area felt so heavy. My baby.

I was four months pregnant when I finally told my boyfriend that I was having his baby. He did not leave me and I was very relieved! One day my grandfather called me to his house to speak about marriage. In our St. Lawrence Island culture, men did not propose back in the day. The clan leaders would usually get together to talk about marriage for their kids or grandkids. My grandfather asked me if I wanted to marry him, I told him I didn't know what to do because of my plans to go to college. I asked him if I had time to think about and he said yes. Two weeks went by and my grandfather called me to his house again. He asked me if I loved him and if I thought he would take good care of me. That's when I decided I wanted to get married. Several months later, my new fiancé's clan people delivered gifts to my grandfather's house. While this was happening, I hid in my bedroom at my parents' house, crying because I was still unsure. I did not want to take part in any of it. I just wanted to hide! I was ready for marriage but at the same time, I wasn't. We do kind of like a dowry tradition when a woman is getting married. Then, the man would do servitude for the girl's clan people, especially for the Elders of the clan. It also meant the man had to provide for the girl's clan, meaning hunt and fish for them. We got traditionally married in May of 1987 before my son was born. In a way, I felt some pride. I wanted to be with him for the rest of our lives.

My son was born on June 2, 1987, in Nome, Alaska. I had to fly to Nome to give birth to him because, you know, no hospitals in the village yet. I waited a couple of weeks before I finally had him. I felt so proud to be his mom! I felt like he was a blessing to us. His dad moved into my parents' house to serve my clan and we call this process "nengaawiqa", meaning servitude for my clan people. We were so happy to have our own family. I was just so happy and filled with joy! My son was named after his uncle on his paternal side.

In December of 1987, when my son was six months old, I was home with my baby and my fiancé. We started to argue but I can't remember what it was about, and the next thing I knew, I was trying to run for my safety. He dragged me by my hair down the hallway and started to kick me all over my body except for my face. He kicked me on my legs, my arms, the top of my head, and especially in my private area. I remember covering my face with my hands. Somehow, I managed to get away and locked myself in the bathroom. He banged on the bathroom door and I wouldn't let him in. I was so scared, especially for my baby who was sleeping on my bed. He was alone in my bedroom, but I was too scared to open the bathroom door. My fiancé eventually gave up and left the house. After he left, I cried so hard laying in a fetal position on the floor and I was in shock. I couldn't believe he did this to me. I went into my bedroom and took my sleeping son and put him on my lap, staring at his face while I was in tears. I tried to cry quietly because I did not want to wake him. I swallowed my tears. I asked myself in my mind, "Is this okay? Is this love? Is this normal?" I was so confused because I had never witnessed men beat women in my life before. I was too ashamed to tell anyone, so I kept it a secret. I did not tell a single person. I had a very challenging time using the bathroom because he kicked me mostly on my private part. I had a dark blue and purple bruise that went all the way up to my belly button. My private area was so swollen and painful. I was in a lot of pain all over my body from the kicks. He came back two days later, begging me to take him back. He told me he didn't know what came over him and that he would never do it again. He told me he loved me and couldn't live without me. I believed him, so I took him back. We were once again happy with our son and I was in love with him. I was proud to be his soon-to-be wife. I started to plan for our wedding and started looking at wedding dresses. It was so exciting!

Months went by and we were still so happy! Until it happened again. He kicked and punched me where nobody could see on my body. He promised me again that it would never happen again. I believed him. It happened again, and again, and again. Every time he beat me, it was always my fault. It was never his fault, according to him. I still kept it a secret. I was still too ashamed to tell anyone and I did not want people to judge him or go against him. It was my way of protecting him. No one needed to know that he beats me.

Eventually, we moved into a one-bedroom house with our three minor children. The beatings continued. I really thought if we moved into our own home that he would stop beating me. I was afraid of him. I had to be careful of what I did or said. I tried not to upset him. I was not allowed to say hello to men or look them in the face without being accused of cheating. If I looked them in the eyes, I received a beating after an accusation.

Four years later, I was still keeping it a secret. He kept threatening that if I left he would find me, kill me and kill himself, and that it would be my fault. He told me that I would never see our children again and that no one would ever love me. I believed everything he said to me. I truly believed it with my whole heart. No one will love me. He will kill me and then kill himself. I will never be able to see my children again. I cannot leave. I stayed. By this time, some people knew what was happening: "Why don't you leave him for the sake of your kids?"

He started punching me in the face. He gave me a broken nose and two black eyes one day. I was very embarrassed to be seen with two black eyes so I wore sunglasses. I hated being out and about when I had bruises on my face. I did not want people to ask me how I was getting my bruises. One day, when I had a black eye, I went to my parents' house and it was just my parents and I. We were all sitting there quietly. My father asked me what happened to me. I said it in one word, "Basketball" without looking at either of my parents. He asked, "Are you sure you get your bruises from basketball?". I couldn't get myself to say anything, so I just cried in silence. My parents didn't really say anything afterwards, but I could feel both of their worries. I think they didn't know what to say because it was too overwhelming for them. I cannot imagine any of my girls experiencing domestic violence, I don't know what I would do, I just know I would be very angry. I would do what I could to protect my girls if anyone ever hurt them. I went home feeling so ashamed of myself. I felt like shit! I felt so unloved and worthless by him. Am I worthy of love and respect? I asked myself many times.

I thought if we became officially married, the beatings would stop. We had a beautiful wedding. It was so fun to decorate for our wedding with the help of my bridal party. I was so happy we were finally going to get married! My father flew to Nome to get me a wedding cake as we had no bakery in the village. I thought that was so very nice of my dad to do that. He truly showed how much he cared about both of us. We got married on February 14, 1989, but the beatings didn't stop after we got married, they only got worse.

My grandfather called me over to his house so I went the next day. He had a message for my husband, "Tell your husband I need to speak to him." I went home and told my husband my grandfather wanted to speak to him, and I got beat for it. I wondered if he ever felt guilt. He reacted angrily because I'm sure now he felt some shame. It was never in my heart for him to be shamed because I loved him so much. Knowing my grandfather, he would not have shamed him, but he would have spoken to him lovingly and forgivingly. My husband did not know my grandfather like I did. I wonder what my grandfather would have said to him? I just know he would remind him of our traditional values that shape us into who we are.

He broke two of my ribs. It was so hard to breathe, sneeze, or cough. It was very painful to speak. He tore some of my clothes, broke my big mirror I got from my parents for my birthday, and broke some of my other personal belongings. I was very afraid of him. He's going to kill me someday. He did everything in his power to avoid being confronted by my grandfather. My grandfather called me over again, "Tell your husband if he does not change the way he treats you, I will take you back." I get beat for it again because it's my fault according to him. It hurt me deeply when he tore my clothes and broke my personal belongings, especially my gifts. He made me feel like I was not valued and that I was not worthy. I felt like I was just trash to him. I did not feel I was worthy of love. What is the point of living? At this point I'm ready to die. I started to have suicidal ideations. In my head, I created all these different scenarios on how to end my life. I could hang myself or I could shoot my head off. I don't think he would care. But what about my kids??!! Every time I thought about my kids, I would change my mind. I can't just leave my kids like that! They were the only reason why I clung to life no matter how much I wanted to kill myself.

He threatened to burn me alive. We had some heating fuel right outside the door. Some people were outside the house trying to talk to him and get him to open the door. He locked me in the house and he wouldn't let them in. He told them through the window if they didn't leave, he was going to burn me alive. I've never been so scared in my life. My whole body shook from head to toe and it felt like my body was cold. They stayed outside our house, trying to convince him to open the door. I don't remember how long they stayed outside our house, but he eventually unlocked the door. I just remember it took him a long time to unlock the door. They spoke to him about the beatings and how he needed to love me the proper way, but it happened again, and again, and again over the months. I was just a punching bag. I felt like I did not matter to him. I was nothing. According to him I was just a bitch, whore, worthless, and good for nothing. I believed him.

This time he put a loaded rifle in my face. There were bags of clothes and he used to prop the rifle on top of them. My whole body shook from fear. He had been out all day and I knew he was out drinking. That was usually the case when he didn't return home all day. He came home intoxicated and in a rage. He told me he was going to kill me first, then kill himself and that it would be my fault. I had never shaken so hard in my life before from fear other than the time he threatened to burn me alive. I felt so weak and powerless. I really thought that was it. I thought I was going to die that night, I truly believed it. I begged him not to kill me or himself. I was tearful but tried not to cry too loud because my babies were sleeping. I did not want them to wake up. I asked him who would raise our children. He pointed the loaded rifle in my face while I was sitting on the bed next to my three sleeping children. What if he shoots me while I sit right next to my sleeping kids? I was so afraid for my babies. He finally decided to put the rifle down. That was the longest 20 minutes of my life! I was so terrified for myself, my children, and for him. I wanted things to be okay and I believed some day he would stop beating me. I had hoped that he would change. That is why I remained and stayed aside from the threats. I believed he would change for us and our children.

Months went by and now years, he still beats me. He broke more of my personal belongings. He did that to use it as a threat and to make me powerless. I got so many countless bruises, especially on my face, from him punching me. I would go to work embarrassed with black eyes. I wore sunglasses to work. I didn't realize how depressed I was. I couldn't laugh, smile, or cry anymore. I didn't know that your emotions can go numb when depressed. I just wanted to die. I didn't know how to feel any more. I felt no emotions whatsoever. I wondered one day why I couldn't feel any more. I just wanted my life to end. Why am I still alive? I am not worthy. I now wanted him to just end my life.

One day, he got on top of me and started choking me. My oldest son was five years old at the time. My son tried to protect me from his dad as little as he was, and he started hitting him from behind, "I promise you when I grow up I will beat you up!". His brother happened to walk in while he was choking me. I was nearly blacked out. His brother held him down and told me to run with the kids. I grabbed my one-month-old baby and my five-year-old son and I ran out the door with no pants or jacket. I held my baby under my t-shirt with a blanket over him and held my five-year-old son's hand while I ran. It was the month of February and it was about -20 outside. I ran to the closest relative's house with my babies. I asked my cousin to lock the door behind me. I was crying frantically. I was afraid at that moment because his brother shouted at me to leave the house with my kids, which triggered me. He was only trying to keep me safe. My husband came banging on the door and yelled, "I know they are in there! Let me in!" I was so terrified. He finally gave up and left. My sons and I stayed the night at my cousin's that night. I was too scared to go home. We went home the next day, and nothing happened. He accused me of cheating on him while I was at my cousin's house. Why would I do that? I love you and I will stay faithful to you!

He beat me again. I'm so depressed and I want my life to end. I was not afraid of him this time. I was done with my life. I called him a name when he called me a name, I punched him back when he punched me, and I kicked him back when he kicked me. I yelled at him, "KILL ME! HURRY UP! WHAT ARE YOU WAITING FOR?! LET'S END IT NOW!" but he didn't kill me. I was so very upset that he wouldn't kill me! I ran out to the shed, knowing he had a loaded rifle. I grabbed the rifle and, got on my knees and put the muzzle in my mouth. I took the rifle off safety, but he came up behind me and grabbed the rifle. I'm surprised the rifle didn't go off. I sat there and cried! I didn't know what to do anymore. I just wanted to die. I wanted him to kill me. "Please! Just kill me!" but he wouldn't do it. "Why won't you kill me?! I'm a nobody."

We eventually moved into a new 4-bedroom house closer to my parents' house through the Bering Straits Housing Authority. Our happiness didn't last very long. One day his cousin was visiting us. We started to argue in front of his cousin but I can't remember what it was about. I went to use the restroom and he barged in behind me. He locked me in the bathroom and started to beat me. My head was hurt because he punched me on my head. I had a bloody nose. His cousin tried to get into the bathroom to help me but he wouldn't open the door. His cousin ended up leaving. I thought maybe he ran to get help, but no one came. He's going to beat me even more I thought. He finally stopped and left the bathroom. I went to the bedroom and I laid down in pain. He gave me another black eye and now my nose might be broken again.

It's been ten years since the beatings began. Over the years, I tried to leave but always ended up going back to him, because he promised me he changed and I believed him every time. I was not afraid of him beating me anymore. I didn't care if he beat me to death because that's what I wanted. Just kill me now, please. I don't want to live anymore. Why won't he just end it?

Chapter Nine

An Angel Saved Me

    One night, I had a dream. I was in a small room with no windows or doors, furniture or decor, but the walls, ceiling and floor were all white marble. I was lying in a fetal position on my left side. I was wearing a white T-shirt and jeans. I was paralyzed from head to toe and I had no emotions. I heard a female humming from a distance but I could not see her. When I finally saw her, she was about a foot off the floor with a baby blue gown on, brunette hair past her knees, and the most beautiful blue eyes I have ever seen in a human to this day! She gently wrapped her hands around my wrists and picked me up. I was limp because I was paralyzed. She wrapped her hands around my waist and held me up. She danced with me and she sang to me so gently and beautifully! Suddenly, my physical sensations and emotions came back! I was crying happy tears in my dream. I was in tears for the first time in many months when I woke up. I sat up and said out loud to myself, "I want to live! I want to live! I want to live!" That was when I decided it was time to leave for good. I suddenly felt strong enough to leave.

    I started creating scenarios in my head on how I was going to leave him. I had a very tough time deciding how and when. What about my kids? I wasn't sure what to do so I went to my grandparents to speak to them because I needed their advice. My grandmother said, "If you leave him, you will not take those kids with you because they do not belong to you, they belong to his clan." Our clan system has protocols; one of them is when children are born and a man and a woman are married, the children are automatically born into the father's clan. My grandfather urged me to leave him. He gave me the go-ahead to leave. He was happy with the decision I made. I did not tell anyone else. I felt my words would be safe with my grandparents.

    I couldn't figure out how I was going to leave. I continued to create scenarios in my head. Just the thought of leaving scared me because I was worried I would never see my children again as he said over the years. What the heck am I to do and how am I to leave? Even at this point and time, I was very confused on what I should really do. I wanted to stay, but I knew in my heart I couldn't stay. I was worried for my kids and I loved them so much that I stayed no matter the beatings over the years. They were the main reason I stayed. I also loved him and I was afraid of being alone.

Chapter Ten

My Mother Apologizes to my Siblings and I

Before I left him, I went to my parents' house. My mother and my siblings were there. My mother apologized to my siblings and I for all the abuse we endured growing up. My siblings and I were silent. Tears were rolling down my cheeks and I couldn't get myself to look up. None of us responded to our mother. I never accepted my mother's apology. I was angry and resentful towards her. I wasn't ready to forgive her so I never accepted her apology. My siblings did not say anything to her either. I don't know what they were thinking or feeling. I believe we had similar feelings.

Many years later (2023) in my sacred space, I journeyed. I saw that I was at the fish camp where I grew up in the summertime. I was urged to go into the body of water to cleanse my entire being. I swam and received cleansing. I was joined by a pool of fish who swam with me. I was then urged to get out of the water. From a distance I saw my mother outside the tent cooking and making fry bread. I went over and sat by my mother. I told my mother that I forgave her for all the abuse. My mother said, "I already knew you forgave me." I asked how she knew. She said, "You showed me." At that moment I realized that all along I did show her I forgave her by doing for her, telling her I love her, checking on her, flying her into Anchorage to be with me, and sending the things that she needed. She knew I forgave her. I could not live with unforgiveness in my heart for my mother. I love my mom, the woman who brought me into this world. I wouldn't want anyone else to be my mom even after what my siblings and I went through.

A few days later I called my mother. I asked my mom if she remembered apologizing to my siblings and I for the abuse. She didn't say anything in return. I let her know that I forgave her. My mother was silent so I told her I loved her. I didn't need to say anything else because she already knew I forgave her. I did not want her to feel uncomfortable. So, I changed the subject to how I felt about my job to steer away from my mom being uncomfortable.

Today my mother and I have a very positive relationship. She calls and texts me daily. If she does not hear from me, she calls or text, she gets worried. So, I try to make it a point to call or text her so she knows I'm okay. We say I love you to each other several times per week. She means so very much to me and I really did forgive her. Whatever happened to her when she was in boarding school was not her fault. I feel very protective of her. My mother needs healing too so we are working towards that. She has hurt in her heart not only from boarding school, but I choose not to share here.

Chapter Eleven

Can I brave leaving now?

    I flew to Anchorage for an annual event called "Alaska Federation of Natives", a 3-day conference. When it was time to go back to Savoonga, I made the hardest decision to stay, as scared as I was. I decided not to call anyone, not even my parents, to tell them that I was not coming home. I didn't know how to not go home, I needed to have some kind of reason to make me stay. I really thought he would fly to Anchorage to look for me. I found an excuse not to go home. I needed to have an excuse other than I did not want to be with him anymore because of my safety. No parent wants their daughter to go through what I did.

    I would sit outside every night and stare at the moon and the stars if there were no clouds. I wondered if my children were staring at the moon and the stars the same time as me. I would sit there and cry, not knowing what to do. I hurt for my children deep inside, and it was very hard to bear. It was one of the most emotional pains I have ever endured. My children. What should I do?

I was still feeling confused about whether I should go back to him or not. I knew if I did, he would probably still hurt me, but my heart wanted to believe he would change. I missed him so much and I loved him. I missed going hunting with him and watching him want to share his catch with Elders and other families. I missed our rides together with our children on our good days. We didn't always have bad days. I missed going to community events with him with our children. I missed cooking Native foods with him. I missed going ice fishing with him. I'm so hurt, but it's unhealthy for us. I had to have the inner strength to not go back to him.

I was dating again, even if I knew I wasn't quite ready. I didn't know how to be alone. I had bad flashbacks and he would try his best to comfort me. A month went by and no one knew where I was. My heart was crushed, especially for my children. I was afraid for myself, afraid for my children, and even afraid for my husband. I finally called my parents' house and my brother answered, "Where are you?! Mom and dad are in Anchorage looking for you!" I went to my aunt's house where my parents were. When I walked in, all three of us hugged and my father said, "My run-away baby" I cried in silence, I didn't know what to say. My tears were a message to them that I had to leave for myself and even my children, that I was strong enough to be away in a world so different than mine, that I could survive in the city even if at times I felt like I couldn't make it, that I am worthy of respect and love, and that I was even helping him without realizing it at that moment and time. He needed healing, too.

I was staying with a man I started dating. I couldn't get a job in Anchorage and I couldn't understand why. I went to countless job interviews and I did not know exactly why no one was hiring me. I blamed it on my skin color when I couldn't find a reason. It made me feel ashamed to be Native. I decided it was time for me to go home after six months of trying to find a job in Anchorage. I couldn't support myself in the city. I made my arrangements to go home. I felt relief, sadness, and worry all at the same time.

I called my parents and asked them to pick me up from the airport. When the plane landed, my husband was standing right outside the airplane. My heart was pounding! It felt like it was going to pound out of my chest and I couldn't get myself to look at him. I was too scared. I walked right past him straight towards my parents. I told my parents to take me to their house. My children were so happy to see me that they climbed all over me and wouldn't leave my side! I was so happy to be united with them again! Soon, my husband walked in and asked to speak to me in private. My heart sunk. I was so scared for my life. I went outside to speak to him in private as scared as I was. I thought I was going to fall to the ground because my legs felt weak and they were shaking. He begged me to return to him and told me he was a changed man. I tried so hard not to cry, but tears rolled down my cheeks. I looked at him and said, "Only if you promise me to never touch me again." he promised he would never hurt me again, but something inside of me said, "No" I looked at him, pointed towards the door, and said, "NO. Leave. I cannot go back to you." he left without saying a word. I fell to my knees and sobbed with my hands over my face. I was relieved for myself but hurt for him at the same time. I loved him and I wanted to be with him, but something inside me said I shouldn't. I suddenly felt some power inside me that I was able to tell him no!

Chapter Twelve

Moving Again

I saved up money as the months went by and decided to give Anchorage another try. I came back and this time I decided to watch white people so I could learn how to fit in. I also wanted to know where I went wrong the first time I tried to live in Anchorage. I went to random public places and sat there and observed white people. As I sat on the bench at Dimond Center Mall, I saw a white woman come around the corner, wearing a dress, high heels, hair put up, and nails made perfect. I asked myself if I needed to dress like her, which terrified me! I grew up with jeans and T-shirts! I watched more white people - how they dressed, how they walked, how they spoke, and their personalities. I observed everything I possibly could about them. I realized my people were the opposite of white people. According to my observations, white people were loud, not ashamed or shy, outgoing, and some would even talk over each other. Where I come from, we don't do that. My grandmother said, "Yakuqlusi – talk quietly amongst yourselves." It was a respectful thing in my culture. I noticed, too, that eye contact is important in Western culture; it means you are paying attention, being honest, and interested in engaging in a conversation. Where I come from, eye contact is a sign of challenge, we use very little to no eye contact. Firm handshakes in the Western culture are a sign of respect. Where I come from, we greet each other with a nod. In the Western culture it is "iMPOrtanT tO sING thE EngliSH LANGuaGE" if you want to be heard. Where I come from, "w e s p e a k a t a s l o w e r p a c e" and we do not use tone. Imagine when I went to these job interviews, how the interviewers probably thought I was rude, not interested, slow and stupid. I now understood why no one hired me. My grandfather said, "It doesn't matter how you say it. What is important is what you mean." Whose style of communication is right? Who is wrong? No one is right or wrong. People need to understand there are many different styles of communication. The Western style of communication is not the only way. Okay. I now know not to go to a job interview in jeans and t-shirts. Where I come from, we come as we are. We don't cover ourselves up to be anything other than ourselves. You want people to get to know the real you. I practiced, and practiced, and practiced so I could be accepted in this second world. I forced myself to speak at a faster rate and to sing the English language. I forced myself to use eye contact and handshakes. I finally landed a job after "Covering up" the real me in a business suit. My thoughts and feelings to this day are that it feels like you are not your authentic self when you wear a business suit to a job interview because you are not showing the real you. At home, you come as you are. Those are just cultural differences and those are my opinions. No matter our cultural background, no one is right or wrong. We each have our own opinions and that's okay.

 When I realized the cultural differences between Western and Yupik cultures, I wrote this paper hoping people would better understand me and my culture. I had to look inside from the outside to see from a Western cultural lens. I titled this writing "Aatak Ayguumun Angwaaghnaqi – Keep Paddling Against the Wind", because the winds are the challenges I faced in my life.:

 "I was born at a time when changes were new at home; no television, telephones, or computers. Some changes were good, and some not so much. We were forced to adapt to the changes upon the arrival of the new people. They created a system foreign to my people and culture.

Many of our traditions were taken away, but some were put to sleep. Some of our traditions were what kept our people healthy emotionally, mentally, physically, and spiritually. However, we are seeing some of our traditions come to life again in this modern-day world.

"I moved to Anchorage, Alaska, in 1997 for several reasons. I was not prepared mentally, emotionally, or spiritually for what was to come. I was frightened when I first arrived to the city. Moving to Anchorage felt like I was moving to a foreign country because the dominant culture's ways were very different from our way of life on St. Lawrence Island. As the missionaries stated we were "Backward people" when they arrived in the villages.

"Some changes were very challenging for me and it took me years to adapt. It was difficult for me to get to know different cultures, but some not so much. It took me several years to adapt to the Western system and communication styles. Although I have not fully adapted to the system yet, I am feeling more comfortable the more I experience. I learned through my observations that they spoke faster, shorter pauses in between, or no pauses at all cutting other people off. We were given many different styles of communication by Creator to use as a tool and not one culture's way of communication is right or wrong. There are differences and we must learn to accept them. Just because one speaks the same tone without pitch, does not mean their style is wrong. Listen to the words they are saying, that's what is important.

"Speaking English is not my strongest communication skill as it is my second language. I am more comfortable and fluent in my Yupik language. As my husband says to me when I can't say something in English, "Say it in Yupik first, then say it in English." Sometimes it's difficult to describe or explain something in English, especially if some of our words don't exist in English. I have challenges when trying to write a paper in college. I work harder than English speakers only.

"I wrote a 20-page paper for one of my college classes. The topic I chose was "Integrating Two Worlds" – Western and Yupik cultures. Integrating Indigenous ways into the Western system would allow for services in the Native community to be more successful. My professor required students to use 15-20 peer-reviewed sources. I used three sources written by Alaska Native people because they were closest related to my Yupik culture. I decided to write from my heart instead of using peer-reviewed sources for the rest. I shared the knowledge passed down by my grandparents and other Elders from my community that our ancestors passed down. I told my husband that I would either receive an F for a grade on my paper or that the university would take what I wrote and use it as a resource. In my writing, I shared, "If the university

can teach mythology and folklore in class, we can teach the natural laws or traditional values of the Alaska Native people. My grandfather had a PhD in Indigenous philosophy. Our culture and traditions were already peer-reviewed by my ancestors."

"I am learning more about myself as I experience Western culture, and being married to a non-Native man, I have discovered new things. I am learning to survive in a world very different from our people. The more I experience, the more I learn, the more I put puzzle pieces together, and the more I understand.

"Living in a world so different from our people made me realize how important it is to teach our people's natural laws or traditional values. It is important to teach about Yuguumalleq, the ways of the Human Being. We are one with our people, one with nature, one with animals, and one with Creator. When we are together, we are stronger. There will come a time when we must come together and work together, even if we don't like our neighbours or co-workers. This is one of our strengths. How do we expect to live together in villages, towns, and cities? It is very important to share our knowledge and the values taught for it makes this world a better place. When different cultures teach each other, we have a better understanding and more respect for each other.

"So many things were done differently that didn't make sense to me when I first moved. I had to crawl out of my skin and force myself to face many challenges and mingle with them. I was forced to familiarize myself and get comfortable with the challenges coming at me so fast and loud! I felt like a lost child in the middle of nowhere. How I missed being on my grandfather's shoulders, so peaceful and content! How is it I went from such a peaceful world to fast paced and loud? I'm okay with it now for the most part. I am now an urbanized Native. It isn't bad as long I remember who I am, what I was taught, and where I come from. I must balance my life and make the best of both worlds.......but did I have to change who I am for me to be accepted in this second world?

"I had to force myself to sing the English language and speak at a rate I was uncomfortable with. My heart and mind would race, and I'd stumble on my words. I would get embarrassed when I didn't know how to put words into sentences and I would freeze, "How do I say it?" I was so afraid to speak English. I didn't want people to make fun of me or look down at me. I used to be scared to even order food from any restaurant. Today I am more comfortable speaking English. My grandfather's quote says, "Whenever you don't know what to say, say what's in your heart. Don't matter how it sounds, what's important is what it means". It helps me feel better when I remember his words.

"I used to be afraid of making new friends of different races, because I only knew what to expect from our people. I was afraid of getting to know what was different than mine. I was afraid of asking questions or being asked questions. I was afraid I wouldn't know how to answer or understand what they were saying. I was embarrassed to let people know my vocabulary was not wide as English speakers only. I didn't want people to think I was slow. However, a woman who also helped me feel better said, "You speak two languages, and your vocabulary is much wider than that of English speakers."

"It was awkward for me to sit next to a non-Native who found silence to be awkward because all I could think of was how the weather is, "It's a beautiful day". Silence is comforting to me. It doesn't matter if you spend time with others in silence, presence is all that matters. We don't need to state the obvious. "How are you?" to me is a filler. People who are awkward with silence tend to ask others how they are doing. So basically, they say, "I don't really want to know how you're doing, but how are you?" Then an Elder tells you everything about themselves and you wonder, "Why are they telling me everything about themselves?" You asked.

"My role as a Yupik woman is to speak my mother's tongue, to pack foods away gathered from the land and sea, to skin sew, to teach the values of our people, to pluck duck, cut fish, to share what I have, and to always know who I am and where I come from. My role as an American citizen is to work Monday-Friday from 9am-5pm, to support my family, and pay my taxes. Which is more important? Both are, because we must balance our lives if we come from more than one culture.

"I remember I was reorganising chairs, and the room was full of teenagers. Not one single teenager offered to help. I was disappointed in myself because I realized that I was part of the fault for not teaching the values of the Native people. We get up to help without being asked, especially our Elders. We knew when to help those in need. That's just the way it is.

"I would hurt for our people when the outside world judged us for our subsistence way of life. People often question us, "Why hunt for seals and whales?" We hunt for seals and whales for the same reason people buy meat from the store, for survival. We must go get our own food because of the lack of employment and this is our way of life, it is ingrained in us. When Creator first made earth, he placed many different animals in every part of the world. You will not find walrus in the waters of New York City, there are no caribou in the lands of Miami, and you will not find reindeer in Salt Lake City. There are no polar bears in Los Angeles, no kangaroos in Nome, and no zebras in Anchorage. The human race did not choose these animals for

themselves, they were chosen for us.

"Having to use handshakes was odd to me when I first moved, when all we do is greet each other with a nod. A firm handshake is a sign of respect in the Western culture. What about those eyebrows? Yes! "I don't know" might mean, "It's up to you," or "I don't want to tell you," or "I don't know how to tell you or put it in words." You will sense it when you understand the differences.

"I have adapted to a certain degree in this second world. Things aren't as foreign as they used to be; however, some things are still foreign. I miss the ocean, I miss the pace, and I miss that community feeling. I am not afraid to speak English anymore. I am not afraid to stand up for myself. I have taught myself how to sing the English language. I have friends all walks of life that I value and appreciate. I have learned so much from them.

"Today I am happy with my city life, but not 100%. It doesn't mean I will stop being Yupik. I will always be Yupik no matter where I go. City life is so much more convenient, but it also spoils people. Everything is available to you and food comes packaged. We don't have to worry about how far out to travel to get our food, being gone for days or weeks, or having enough hunting tools and partners. It is much harder at home. I appreciate all our hunters and providers. They take care of all of us and make sure no one goes hungry by sharing with families in the community."

I came up with this visual in hopes especially non-Indigenous people would understand some of us Indigenous people. We may have some differences in our communication styles even in our Native community, but this is in general.

P-A-C-E

Some people raised in the villages speak at a much slower pace. Sometimes there is a long pause in between words. Some people find this pace to be awkward. There is a reason why there is a long pause. Those that speak at a faster pace may think those who speak at a slow pace as slow and unintelligent.

VOLUME

Some Alaskan Native people are soft-spoken. They are uncomfortable speaking loud. They may find speaking loud as being disrespectful or being disruptive. Those who are soft-spoken may find people who speak loud obnoxious and annoying.

The People Who Speak Loud May Find People Who Are Soft-Spoken As Shy And Anti-Social.

PITCH

Some alaska native people raised in the villages often do not use pitch when they are speaking. the only thing that matters is that you get your words across. when english was taught to the villagers the non-natives did not teach the importance of pitch of the western culture. **wESTERners USe pITCH. IF yOU do NOT Use pITCH, yOU wILL Put otherS to SLEEP. CONverSAtion BeCOMES less iNTERestING.**

1997

Chapter Thirteen

I Need Help

I knew I needed help because of all the trauma I endured from my past since my childhood. I decided not to seek help, because I was worried I would end up with another counselor who wouldn't understand me or my culture. Without even realizing it, I began to drink alcohol to numb my pain because I didn't know how to deal with it. I didn't want to feel my feelings and I didn't know how to cope with them. I started off as a weekend drinker, to every other day, and eventually every day. I don't know how I made it to work every day with two to four hours of sleep most nights. I couldn't stay away from alcohol and marijuana because I used it as a coping mechanism. It turned into an addiction without realizing it.

I then went to my boyfriend's village to live with him there. I really enjoyed being there with him and his family. I made great friends while I was there. I also enjoyed eating their kind of traditional foods. We may eat some of the same foods, but they also have different cultural foods. I got pregnant with our son. I'm glad I decided to quit drinking when we decided to try for a baby. I loved going through this pregnancy with him. I was so happy and I felt so safe with him. I loved watching him put his hands over my belly when the baby was moving. He often talked to our baby while I carried him. I knew he would be a great dad.

We flew to Anchorage to have our son. We stayed at his sister's apartment. We spent a lot of time at my cousin Barb's so I could sew with her and eat our traditional foods from home. Barb is more like a sister to me. I spent my summers in Gambell at Barb's parent's house. Her dad was my uncle on my father's side. My grandfather told me I needed to know who my family and extended family were. He urged me to be close to the Apangalook's.

I finally went into labor and our son was born on April 29, 1999. We were so happy for our new son! It was a joy for me to be in a healthy relationship without worrying about getting physically hurt. I knew in my heart that everything would be good.

We decided to stay in Anchorage instead of returning to Shaktoolik where my boyfriend was from. After some months went by, my son became colicky. He had a bad case of eczema. We took him to get his skin tested at Providence Hospital. It turned out he was allergic to anything with corn, and literally everything has corn! I had to do a lot of label reading while I breastfed him because he would flare up if I consumed anything with corn.

When my son turned two years old, I started drinking again. This time I was worse than before. I was careless. By this time his father and I were no longer together. It bothered me in my heart knowing that he could be with someone else, but we needed to be apart. My past trauma re-emerged because I had never received the help that I needed. I was going through a lot at that time. What am I to do? I had to take it one day at time, but I didn't know how to sit with my past trauma and I didn't know how to cope with it.

As the years went by and my son was older, he was more aware of my drinking problem. His father and I got back together. My son spent weekends with his grandparents. As small as my son was, he encouraged me to quit drinking. He told me I had a drinking problem at the age of seven. At his young age, my son knew the dysfunctional lifestyle I was living. Of course, I denied it and ignored him because I didn't want to hear it. He was the only one in my family who encouraged me to quit drinking and even pointed out why I shouldn't drink. I felt some guilt, but I couldn't stay away from alcohol. It was my unhealthy coping mechanism.

The years went by, my drinking problem got much worse. I got charged with driving under the influence of alcohol on October 10, 2007. The judge gave me three years' probation, lost my driver's license for 90 days, and the court ordered to go to treatment. Whatever! I don't have a drinking problem! I was angry at the judge because in my addictive mind, nothing was my fault. The judge was at fault all the way. I did not want to be held accountable. IT WAS NOT MY FAULT! I was selfish and stubborn and didn't want any accountability. Little did I know that in the future, I would be grateful for the judge, serving time, being in treatment, and being held accountable.

My niece found out she was pregnant. I asked to adopt the baby. I wanted so badly to adopt in the past. We ended up adopting her and my son named her "Allyssa". I asked the hospital to give me a separate room with my baby. I was afraid my niece would change her mind. I had attempted to adopt three other times. I was so in love with our new baby! I was so very grateful that she was ours to raise. Dats my baby girl. I slowed my drinking down after she was born, but it didn't last long. I was an alcohol addict and I wasn't ready to admit that I was.

I hired a babysitter every weekend so I could go out to drink at Gaslight in downtown Anchorage. Everyone knew me there. It was my bar. Not long after we adopted our baby girl, their father and I split up. He stayed sober while I was drinking. Our kids stayed with him majority of the time because I was too busy drinking.

I moved into an apartment where my drinking became worse than ever. I was drinking every day. I had people over at my apartment to drink with me. Sometimes we would wait until 10:00 AM for the liquor store to open so we could drink some more, because we did not have enough from the night before. One bottle of a fifth of hard liquor was not enough for the night. My brother was there too. He would do the alcohol runs for me when the liquor  store opened. My brother also had a drinking problem. We drank together every night. All that mattered to me was that I had a drink and my brother to drink with me too.

One night when I went to Gaslight, a new security guy was at the door. He carded me and I was annoyed because the security never carded me there because I was a regular. My first words to him when he carded me, "Must be new huh?" I could tell he was  annoyed because he did not look at me or say anything. He handed my card back to me and I went on my to drinking and dancing.

I tried a few times to get my two youngest kids to come be with me at my apartment, but I could not stay sober. As soon as my kids went to sleep, I would start drinking. Some nights I woke my son up and he would be disappointed in me. My son would be in tears, begging me to stop drinking. I decided it was 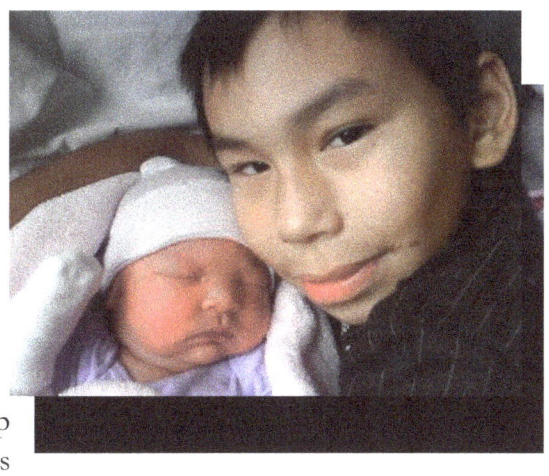 better for my children to be with their dad, because I could not take care of them. I couldn't even take care of myself. I saved my money for alcohol. If I used it for rent, bills, or food, it meant I wouldn't have enough money for alcohol. I chose alcohol over everything else. Eventually, I got evicted from my apartment because I was not paying rent. I lost everything I had except for some clothes I owned. The landlord held my belongings for me to pick up later, but I did not. All I cared about was my next drink.

Sometimes I went to an after-hour party with other people at some stranger's place. As soon as bar break hit, many of us would be out back looking for a house party. I would go with some friends and drink some more. Some days I didn't know whose shoes I ended up with, or  wondered how I got to so-and-so's place from the house party, or who is this guy? It was so disgusting, but I did not care because all I wanted to do was drink. Alcohol was my life and nothing else mattered. Why did I get this far?! I was disgusted with my behavior, but I did not show it and I did not talk about it.

Chapter Fourteen

My New Boyfriend

I played pool league on the Gaslight's pool team so I was there a few days per week. The new security guy was working on the nights I played pool in the league. We became friends and we were very playful with each other. I really liked his personality but I wasn't ready to date. I also thought he was too popular and I didn't want to be with anyone who got too much attention. I secretly watched him from a distance without trying to reveal that I really liked him. I just couldn't date yet.

As the weeks went by, my best friend Tiffany would point at guys at the bar, "What about him?" I kept telling her no and that I wasn't ready to date. She pointed at the new security guy and I

My children Shenise Kingeekuk, son Brandon Asicksik (far right) and my stepson Matthew Johns.

said, "No! He's too popular. He gets too much attention." Several weeks later, she pointed at him again, but I said no again. Several weeks go by and she pointed at him AGAIN. I told her no again. I paused, thought about it, and said, "Maybe I should ask for his number." I was so scared to be rejected but I braved it and asked for his number. He gave me his number! My heart was beating so hard and fast!

I decided I didn't want to initiate anything so I waited for him to call or text me first. Two weeks later he finally texted and he asked me if I wanted to visit him and his son so I went. I was nervous because I liked him so much and even nervous about meeting his son! That is how it all started. He made the first move and I really liked that.

We were seeing each other a couple of times per week. The days I didn't see him I thought about him a lot. I really liked him a lot because he was wise and logical, like my dad. We didn't really become a "Fling thing" right away because he told me he didn't want the boyfriend title yet. We both let things happen naturally.

We were now a girlfriend and a boyfriend. I really liked him so much. One day he said, "You know, I used to watch you secretly." my eyes got so big and I said, "I used to watch you secretly!" Knowing he felt the same way about me was such a really good feeling. My best friend Joy liked him too and hoped the best for me, but at the same time she told me to be careful because she didn't want to see me hurt. She was always protective of me.

Joy somehow always knew when something was wrong with me. She would call, text, or send me memes that were related to what I was going through. I would always ask her how she knew. She just knew! Tiffany was the same. I spent a lot of time with her during the week at her place with her children. Both of my best friends watched people around me because they were protective. How did I get so lucky to have two blue-eyed, blonde-haired, fair-skinned best friends?! I was not going to let some chic take them away from me as my best friends! I was the one that held the best friend title to both of them! I honestly did not want to share them with others.

When I felt emotional, my new boyfriend realized I didn't know how to express myself. He looked at me and said, "It's okay for you to talk about your feelings to me. I will listen." I never heard anyone say that to me before. I didn't know how to express myself. I told him about all the abuse I endured before I moved to Anchorage. When I cried, I couldn't tell him my deepest hurts and my past trauma. Eventually, I was comfortable enough to start expressing myself to him. He gave me a safe space to share my thoughts. He was angry about all I endured. There were times he sat with me and cried with me. I have never seen a man just sit there and cry with me until now.

My three-year probation ended, I was charged with another DUI. I was blacked out drunk that night at a bar in town. My friend took my car key from me. I don't remember going through her purse while she was in the restroom looking for my car key. I took off in my car while very intoxicated. I woke up in Anchorage Jail the next day in a blue uniform. I wasn't sure what happened. I asked an officer and she told me I crashed into a tree and that the police had to break my side window because they couldn't wake me up. They dragged me out of my car and took me to Anchorage Jail. I went to court the next day and the judge said he couldn't arraign me because I was still intoxicated. My blood alcohol level was .438. I could have died thousands of times over.

The next day, I was arraigned and the judge gave me 180 days, 5 years' probation, and the court ordered me to go to treatment. I was angry at the judge. I was transported to Hiland Mountain Correctional Center. I was inmate number 517308. I had no name and no face, I was just a number and a statistic. No one cared about me at Hiland. I was a nobody. They placed me in North Wing, House 2, where inmates were serving short term. I saw my cousin there, and she told me I was on my own and that no one had my back. That's just the way it was. I prepared myself for this by observing all the inmates in my wing, so I knew who to stay away from. My first day in the house I was in, I sat quietly at the table observing the inmates. A young white girl approached me and asked me why I was so quiet. All I could think of telling her was, "I'm just watching people.". She told me that people called me crazy and I asked her why. She said it was because of the tattoos on my chin.

Soon, I started to have a lot of anxieties and my heart was beating all kinds of crazy! I went to the nurse because I felt so sick. She gave me medication and told me it would help. It was to help me with withdrawals. Oh gosh! I was having so much anxiety. I tried really hard to hide my anxiousness from other inmates because I was worried they would target me if they saw it as a weakness.

I became friends with the white girl who approached me. She taught me everything I needed to know about how to be an inmate, what to do, what not to do, who not to speak to or be around, how some officers were bullies, and what not to say. It was a lot to take in and it made me nervous. I was scared for me. I felt like I needed to be extra cautious and I felt like even the walls, ceilings, and floors were watching me.

When I called home, my father asked me if I wanted to be bailed out and I said no. I wanted to stay in there and pay for the wrong I did. By this time, I was homeless. I lost my car, apartment, and everything else I had in the apartment and did not care. I.just.wanted.a.drink. Even if I did not care about losing everything, I wanted to serve time so I could be held accountable.

I called my boss, told him what happened, and asked him if I would lose my job. He told me he would fight to keep me, and he did. I was very lucky I didn't lose my job. Three of my bosses came to visit me while I was serving. The inmates asked me, "What the heck do you do for work and why are your bosses visiting you?!" When I spoke to my two youngest children's father, he told me that some wanted to visit me from work. I was surprised they came to see me too. It made me feel really good that they came to visit me. See Yaari, people really do care about you! I was so grateful they came to visit me.

I forgot to tell my family that if anything bad happens to not tell me, because I couldn't do anything about it while I was serving. I called my children's father and he asked if I heard anything from home. I knew right away something bad happened. I asked him not to tell me who, but what. He said, "Suicide". I hung up on him in panic. I called my best friend and she told me I needed to call him back and ask him who. As hesitant as I was, I called him back, "Don't tell me a name, but whose child?"he said, "Your sister's." I hung up on him and I don't remember what happened next. Next thing I knew, I was on the floor in tears and other inmates surrounded me, trying to comfort me. I was feeling very anxious and helpless. I felt like I couldn't breathe. I asked the officer to speak to the chaplain, but it was a Sunday and it was his day off. The officer came to get me from my wing and told me the chaplain had come to see me. He walked me to the chaplain's office. I called my father's house and he answered. I could hear everyone crying in the background. I asked my father how everyone was doing, and he said, "Not good. Here, speak to your sister." I did not want to speak to her but it was too late. All my sister could say was, "I lost my son." She told me our dad kept calling my nephew's phone hoping he would answer, but he isn't answering. Dad, he's gone. He's dead. I'm sorry. I was very angry at myself because I couldn't be there with my family, especially with my sister. I felt extremely helpless and I hated myself! I couldn't even go home for my nephew's funeral. I had requested to go home for his funeral but it was denied. I was very guilty that I couldn't be at home for my nephew's funeral. My heart was broken into a million pieces.

While I was serving time, I decided to start writing a book. I wrote all day, every day. The inmates found out I was writing. They wanted me to write about them so I did. I wrote everything I saw, tasted, smelled, felt, and witnessed. I went to an officer and asked him to move me to another house. He said he couldn't move me, but he told me to pack my box two days later. He moved me to House 1, where inmates were serving long term. Most of the inmates in that house were young white girls, a black woman, and an older Native woman. They put me in the room with the Native lady. I immediately experienced racism, but I didn't care. The girls gave me a reason to write, and that's exactly what I wanted. I remember one girl came to our door, sprayed perfume, and said out loud that our room was "Stank". So much hate from those girls and they didn't even know me or my roommate.

I remember while in the cafeteria, a woman asked me to bring her fruit to our house. I asked her if it would get me in trouble. My heart said not to do it so I refused. I then remembered the girl who taught me how to be an inmate who told me that I should never do that because, yes, it would get me in trouble. I gave her the nickname M&M because of her first and last name initials. I grew close to her while I was there. I felt so much respect from her.

The girls in our house would argue and shout at each other daily! I was getting so tired of hearing them. I was always the quiet one. I minded my own business and stayed away from all the drama. Even having one strand of hair in the shower would set an inmate off! One day, I got so tired of hearing them argue that I started yelling at them. Everyone was quiet. When I was done yelling, one said, "Yaari! I never thought you would ever yell at anyone!" I told them I was sick of them arguing daily.

There was this female officer whom everyone knew was a bully. She was not nice at all. Just one of those people who took advantage of their authority. I fell asleep sitting up on the couch when she came in and WHACK! She hit the back of the couch with her baton, "WHO SAID YOU COULD SLEEP ON MY COUCH?!!!" She took our microwave away. If an inmate did something they are not supposed to do, something would be taken away from our house. It could be the TV remote, coffee, microwave, or even phone privilege.

I remember while I was in there, I missed the color pink. I did not even like pink at that time. I also missed stop signs and red lights and didn't even like driving. I missed seeing receipts in shopping bags, yet I hated shopping. It meant I was stuck at Hiland. Everything was black, white, and gray inside Hiland. I missed drinking!

While serving, my ex-boyfriend brought my two kids to see me. It hurt me deep inside for my kids to see me like this. I really loved it when they visited me. I played with them and read to them, and loved them up as much as I could. It felt good to spend time with them soberly. It took for me to be locked away to stay sober and visit with them soberly. It was so hard when visiting hour was over and I had to watch them leave. I cried every time they left. I was so grateful that their dad allowed them to visit me. My best friends Joy and Tiffany came to see me too. It felt so good to have them both visiting me there. Joy looked at me and said, "You're not supposed to be here." I knew what she meant by that in my heart. What's done was done and I was serving time for the wrong I did. I was hoping this experience would "Wake me up". I could feel the pain I caused Joy, she truly cared about all of me, not just a part of me. That's why she is one of my best friends. Joy and I grew up together at home. I, too, felt the same way about her. I will not let anyone hurt her. I am protective of her.

While I was at Hiland, I did my best not to swing my hips while I walked because I did not want attention from women. I consciously walked as straight as I could. I had nothing against women who liked other women, it's just that I was into men. I do not judge people's preferences because it's not my place to judge. I was naturally an accepting person.

Finally, when I got out, I kissed the ground! My children's father picked me up with them. I was so happy to be united with my children! I went to his house, took a shower and went to work. I walked into our morning meeting and asked our summer interns if they knew where I've been. One yelled, "Vacation!" I decided to tell the youth the truth. I shared with them my story of the abuse I endured for years. I told them that it was important to seek the help when needed instead of using unhealthy coping mechanisms such as alcohol. I talked about the importance of mental health and healing. Everyone in the room was silent. Some were quietly in tears. I knew I needed to tell them the truth, because I wanted to use it as a teaching tool.

I had to sign an agreement with the Alaska Native Heritage Center saying that I would go through treatment and sober up for at least five years. If I broke my agreement, I would lose my job. I was court-ordered to go through treatment again and I wasn't ready to. I was angry at the judge. Damn! I can't stay away from drinking, yet I told the youth the importance of healthy coping. I didn't know how to quit and I didn't feel I had the strength. I honestly thought I would never quit drinking.

I broke up with my boyfriend from Gaslight because I chose alcohol over him and my kids. I didn't want to see him hurt anymore. I hurt him a lot when I was drinking and he had to take care of me many times while I was intoxicated. He had so much patience for me. He did mention to me that he did not want to be with someone with a drinking problem. He just didn't have it in his heart to break-up with me. I missed him so much, but I knew it was better if we split so I wouldn't hurt him anymore. By the way, his name is Marq. He still watched over me when I was at the bar drinking. He would come to check on me and put his flashlight on my eyes to determine if I had enough to drink. He would signal the bartenders and servers to quit serving me alcohol. He didn't know that I had a bottle in my purse just in case he made them stop serving me. Eventually, he caught on and started checking my purse on my way into the Gaslight. Ugh! I was so annoyed with him.

I was on the waitlist to start treatment. I finally started at Jet Morgan's downtown Anchorage. I lied in my assessment because I did not want to go to residential treatment. If I went to long-term residential treatment, I was afraid I would lose my job. My ex-boyfriend Marq picked me up wherever I was, dropped me off at treatment, picked me up when I was done and dropped me off wherever I needed to go three times per week. I could see he truly cared about me. I remember one day after he dropped me off at treatment, I said out loud to myself, "I will marry him someday!" but how would I marry him? I broke up with him.

On my first night of outpatient treatment on January 5, 2012, I decided to really give it a shot. I listened to the instructor as he gave us an assignment. He said, "When you go home tonight, I want you to look in the mirror and ask yourself these questions. Do you like the choices this person makes? Do you like their lifestyle? Do you like what you see? I want you to pretend you are looking at someone else." I don't have a home, I was a couch surfer. I mostly stayed with my ex, on his couch. He didn't have to do that for me but he did. I closed my eyes and I imagined standing in front of a mirror. When I saw my image in the mirror, I pretended I was looking at someone else. I immediately became judgmental of her. I realized how much damage and hurt I've caused. I suddenly hated myself. I was ashamed and guilty. That was the moment I decided to quit drinking. My mind, heart, and spirit were made up to quit! I knew that was it, but I knew I was going to have a rough time ahead of me because I'd been there before. I called my son, who was 12 years old, who always encouraged me to quit drinking, "Son, I just wanted to let you know I quit drinking. Do you remember those times you encouraged me to quit and I acted like I didn't hear you?" My son said yes. "I heard everything you said, I just wasn't ready to quit. The more you said to me, the closer I was to quitting drinking. Thank you for not giving up on me and thank you for encouraging me to quit. I quit drinking." My son was so happy and relieved. He told me to keep it up.

After I quit drinking, I made some changes and made new boundaries for myself. I changed my phone number, quit going to the bars, asked my drinking buddies not to contact me to drink, and I made a promise to myself that if I felt tempted to drink I would immediately tell someone close to me. My son kept telling me daily how proud of me he was. I was so grateful to him for being such a big support at his young age.

I asked my ex-boyfriend Marq to babysit for him on the weekends to help me stay sober and he agreed. He picked my children and me up every Friday so I could babysit while he worked nights at Gaslight. I went through crazy alcohol withdrawals. I felt so sick, kept having anxieties, and temptation to drink, and my heart was beating irregularly. He put up a punching bag for me to help me through my emotions. He would stand next to me while I cried and punched the bag. When I was done punching the bag, I would turn around and he would just hold me until I was done crying. He would even go on walks with me when I felt I needed to walk temptation out. I went through a very rough time. He stayed by my side even after I broke up with him. I continued to babysit for him every weekend and maintained my sobriety. One weekend of babysitting turned into one week, then it turned into two weeks, three weeks. I looked at Marq and said, "I've been here too long. Can you please drop me off?". He said, "No. We are going to pick your stuff up. You are going to move in with me." I didn't know exactly what to say, but in my heart, I was happy. I loved him and I missed being in a relationship with him. This is how we got back together.

I couldn't believe I actually stayed sober for 30 days, 90 days, six months! I didn't realize I had a lot of fight inside me. I never thought I

would ever be able to quit! Wow! I'm doing it! I felt so good. I had my moments with the urges and temptations, but I worked through them with my loved ones around me. My boyfriend Marq and my son Brandon were my biggest supports. My best friend Joy too. I would immediately tell Marq or Joy any time I felt the urge to drink. I cried and felt angry whenever I felt tempted to drink because I did not want to pick up a drink again, because if I did, it would be harder for me to quit again. I worked too hard to let go! I continued to work through the urges with support. Over time, it started to get easier. I prayed, and prayed, and prayed, asking for willpower and guidance. I asked that a protective shield would be placed around me to keep me from temptation.

After a month and five days of not drinking, I decided to quit smoking too. Ugh! It was rough! I used nicotine patches and it helped

(Left) mother Esther Nuqna Toolie, (middle) late father Herman Pegetkaq Toolie and (right) mother-in-law Carlene Walker.

me. I was so conditioned to have a cigarette after every meal and everything else in between. I became an angrier woman! I remember I joined my best friend and her boyfriend at the time at a bar at Captain Cook. An intoxicated woman was being rude and saying mean things to us. I was highly irritated with her, "Look, lady! I just quit smoking so you better stop it!" She finally left. I was boiling inside and wanted to have a cigarette so badly. About two weeks after I quit smoking, my boyfriend said that maybe I should try to quit smoking another time. I said to him, "No! I worked too hard to get to this point! I won't turn back!" I definitely put in some fight. I fought for myself so I could be alive, especially for my children.

When our relationship became serious, I told him that men do not propose in our culture. He asked what he needed to do. I told him that his father, uncle, and him would have to fly to my village and speak to my father and my uncles. One day, I came home from work and he told me that his son told him something, and I asked what. He said, "So Matthew told me you wanted to marry me." I could feel my face get really hot and red! "I never said that! I really didn't! He asked me what I would do if you proposed!" I was so embarrassed! That same night we ended up talking about marriage. He didn't propose to me but asked me what my thoughts were. After talking about it for some time, we decided to ask our parents what they thought. He called his parents while we waited for mine to arrive in Anchorage.

My parents flew into town and he saw an opportunity to ask for permission from my father to marry me. The two men spoke in private in my parents' room. He had already asked my adult children and they all blessed him to marry me. My father shared with him about my past and how I was abused in my first marriage. He promised my father that day he would take good care of me.

My father gave him the blessing to marry me.

Chapter Fifteen

Spirituality

After being sober for a couple of years, I met some Alaska Native Traditional Healers in Anchorage. They asked me to share my personal experiences and stories of the "Unseen," and I shared everything as far back as I could remember. When I was finished sharing, one of the Elders said, "Did you know in traditional times, you would have been known as a shaman?" I went home crying because I learned the practice was "Evil" and banned by the church. My husband agreed that it was evil and he urged me to stay away from the Elders. I became very curious about the Elders' stories so I decided to meet them again. The more I visited with them, the more I learned, the more I realized the church stigmatized our Native cultures. I continued to visit with the Elders but with caution. One of them offered to take me on a healing journey from my past trauma and I agreed. I met with her virtually once per week for nine months. I experienced more and more of the unseen. I heard, saw, and felt with my third eye and my spirit. I received guidance and healing messages that were meant for me and/or my loved ones. I experienced both good and bad spirits. I would hear Creator speak to me and guide me to do something in life. I always obeyed when I was urged to do something, "And so I shall." The Creator was always right. I realized after nine months of my healing journey that these ancient practices once kept our ancestors healthy. I realized that this was exactly what I needed to heal my broken spirit from my past traumas. I wanted to start doing the people's work, be of service to others, and be a part of bringing healing into the community.

One day, my husband asked me to spend time with him and ride with him to the Dimond Mall to pick up a job application and I agreed. As we were leaving through the garage door, I heard a voice tell me to take my car. So, I told my husband I would drive behind him in my car. He said, "What's the point? I wanted you to ride with me so I could spend time with you." I asked him to trust me. I drove behind him on the highway and I realized he was suddenly not in front of me. I parked outside the mall and he called me, "Where are you?" I told him I was parked outside the mall and I asked him what happened. He said, "My wheel came off." All I said to him was, "I told you so." One day we walked into the house and my husband asked me if I could feel what he did. I told him I did. He asked me what it was, and I said, "It's our son." He asked me if it were a good thing or a bad thing. I told him, "It's just about a girl." We knocked on my son's door and he told us to come in. I asked my son if he had something to tell us, he said no. I reminded my son he could not hide anything from me and I asked him if it was about a girl. "Alright! Alright! Alright! I started dating this girl!" As soon as I laid my eyes on her picture, I knew they wouldn't last long, but I didn't tell my son. A month later, my son said he broke it off with her and I told him I knew they wouldn't last.

As time went on, I experienced more. I began to understand the roles of our ancient shamans through these Alaska Native Elder traditional healers. I now understood what some of my grandfather's teachings were. In his own way, he told me that thinking good thoughts of others was a form of prayer. I also learned giving others good energy was a form of prayer and healing. It is important to use good energy in our everyday lives, to think good thoughts of others, and to be careful with our words. My grandfather told us never to wish illness or bad thoughts about others.

I often wondered how I could feel other people's energies over the years. I could feel their emotional, mental, physical, and spiritual being. When people lie to me, I can pick it up right away, or when they are trying to cover something up. I could feel their physical, emotional, mental, or spiritual pains. I am able to see into their future or their past, but not all the time. Their personalities are revealed to me. I can sense injuries and sometimes can see them like x-ray eyes. Maybe not as clear as an x-ray, but I could see. Sometimes, my hands get very hot, and I call them "Activated hands" meaning someone needs a healing touch. I learned to use my hands to relieve people of pain. I can use my hands to pull pain, illnesses, or bad energy out of people. Sometimes, I do long-distance healing work. My guides show me what to do and how I need to do the work. No healing sessions are ever the same. Some techniques are generally the same based on their needs. I could see, feel, and sense lost spirits or sometimes even evil spirits. The Elders say to never fear evil spirits because you could give them power. Most of the time, I do not acknowledge them when they are near me, but sometimes I speak

to them and let them know I am not afraid.

One day, we were getting ready to do a dance performance at my workplace. I used the restroom before the performance. I put my dance gloves on the sink on the left-hand side. No one was in the restroom except for me. As I was getting ready to go into one of the stalls, I heard a voice tell me to "Pee with the stall door open." I spoke out loud and said, "I am not going to use the bathroom with the stall door open. I don't want anyone to see me." I proceeded to use the restroom and when I was done, I opened the stall door and found my gloves on the floor under the sink. I picked up my gloves and looked to my right, "I am not afraid of you, I am a child of God." I went on stage and danced with the gloves on. After the dance performance, I felt all kinds of negative emotions for two straight days in my heart-center area. I was very sad, depressed, angry, jealous, and hateful for no reason. I called one of the Elder Traditional Healers and she reminded me that I knew what I needed to do to get rid of the heaviness in my heart. She told me an evil spirit attacked me. I went into my sacred space with a glass of water. I went into meditation and prayer. I used the waterfall technique to help get rid of the heaviness. I invited the healing white light to fill my entire being. I formed a protective shield before I journeyed into the spirit world to cleanse my spirit. I received some healing and some guidance from my ancestors.

Over the years, after learning from Elder Traditional Healers, I wrote my experiences so I could use them for reflection. I also did not want to forget the healing messages and guidance from my ancestors and Creator. I also received messages from other spirits such as the wind, a mountain, the fog, the ocean, animal spirits, and trees. No, I am not psychotic. Below are some of my experiences:

In my Sacred Space - December 7, 2016

My grandfather came forward with messages. I am to give all my deepest hurts to the Creator, and Creator will turn them into something greater than I know and will allow me to carry it in my spirit to share with others. After this message was received, I felt peace and love so pure. I wish I had a way to describe the purity I felt. I was reminded to live the values he and my grandmother taught me. I was reminded I needed to forgive myself.

I saw grass moving like waves and they transformed into my ancestors (no gender). I asked my ancestors what messages they had for me. I was reminded to be gentle and kind. I was reminded to live and breathe the values taught to me by my grandparents.

A bowhead whale came forward with messages. I learned from the bowhead whale that it is the most peaceful being on earth that we as humans must live more at peace like them. The bowhead whale said that it is a gift to us from Creator and it gives itself to the people. They said the purpose for its existence is to teach humans about living at peace and that it provides its flesh to our people. With its flesh comes the values of sharing, community, working together, love, and peace.

In My Sacred Space – My First Journey

I was taken to a peaceful location in front of the ocean on a beach. In the horizon, I saw a small, bright light. The sea was very calm and glossy. I could see for miles and miles. The light began to move in my direction and as it came closer, it became bigger and brighter. The light stops in front of me and it was my Apa! I was so happy he came to see me as tears flowed down my face. I asked him why he came to see me, "I want you to know I am always with you. Grandmother and the others are also on the other side and they are doing well."

I felt so much warmth coming from him. His warmth surrounded me with so much love. I sensed our ancestors behind me. I asked him what messages he had for me, "Continue to work for the people. I will be with you and work alongside you and our ancestors will be there too".

I was about to walk on a path to return and I asked him if he wanted to go with me on my journey, he said yes. I came to a gate where my sacred symbol was a naniq (seal oil lamp). I opened the gate and we walked together.

I found myself in a small, white, bright room. There were two large white wings in the air. My Apa put one wing on his left side on himself, and he put one on my right side. I asked him what the wings were and why he gave me only one. He said he wanted me to be like an angel and help others, give messages to people with words from Creator and our ancestors, and use my hands to heal people. He encouraged me to use my gifts from Creator with all I have within me. He said I would know when to use my gifts on people because Creator would let me know when, where and said to me, "And I will guide you always."

I went back on my path towards the ocean. The ocean was bigger. I was asked to go to the water's edge and there I saw my cup, which looked like a Styrofoam cup. I picked it up, filled it with sacred water, and drank a full cup. When I drank the water, it felt like cool air was inside me. I was asked to get into the water and soak myself where I received what felt similar to a baptismal ceremony. WOW! It felt so pure! As I was swimming in the sacred water, I could see black ink like energy leaving my body that was healing for my mind, body, heart, and spirit. When the water cleared and the healing was complete, I came out of the water and looked at the reflection looking back at me. I saw in the reflection shiny round eyes. The face was of an old female Elder in her late 90's. She was smiling at me and seemed happy. She shined with white light. I asked her if she had any messages for me. She told me, "Spread love and peace when you speak to people. When you speak of love and peace, you will share our traditional values to all people. Start with the youngest people first, then move onward with the older generation." The Elderly woman told me that she was my "Higher self" and that I was connected to Creator who guides me in life along with my Apa. I asked her who she was, "I am you, you are me." I thanked her as she gave me a slight bow and she left.

I was then asked to find a dwelling. I found myself in front of a nenglu (sod house) of our ancestors. There was a basket waiting for me in the middle of the floor. There was a rock like object illuminated with a healing white light. I asked the light what it was for, "You are to spread love with it. You are to invite people over for dinner and your cooking will spread love and the light will help you to do that." The light told me that it was the beginning for me to open the heart for the real work to begin with people. I asked the white light where it wanted to live in my body, "In your heart" When the light moved into my heart, I felt it throughout my entire body! I felt so much Creator's love and the WHOLE ROOM lit up so very bright! It felt like I was going to explode from it!

I stepped outside and realized I was at my workplace in front of the lake, and across the lake was the Alaska Native Heritage Center. My apa was in front of me and our ancestors surrounded both of us. Our ancestors had no gender but I could see them as ivory figurines. I asked why I was brought to my workplace, "Your grandmother and I, and our ancestors will work alongside you as you teach about our traditional values to all people. You are to speak of the true history of the people with peace and love, no anger. We want you to help people to forgive those who have harmed people in the past. You won't be doing this alone. You will be strengthened by teaching others. Our Creator will always be by your side as you do your work."

I thanked my Apa and our ancestors for guiding me and for their messages. I turned away and walked alone to my sacred stairs to return.

In my Sacred Space – 2nd Vision

I sat down and began to meditate, pray, and send the Creator's healing white light. I opened my heart and began to send love to my friend, immediately, she put up a shield to keep love from entering her spirit. No matter how much love I tried to give her, she blocked it. I discovered not everyone is ready to receive; therefore, the healing white light of Creator's love returned to me 10-fold. The love I received was so overwhelming and healing to my entire being.

Next, I sent it to my 21-year-old son doing the same process as I did before. I filled up my spirit and sent the light to my son. He immediately soaked it up! He bathed in it and had a blast! He was ready and willing to take it all in. He danced and rejoiced in it! His spirit was ever so bright with a white light.

I then moved on to my oldest daughter. At first, she was a little protective; however, she eventually took in the energy. I could see a green aura light around her. I moved on to my 16-year-old son. He took it all in smoothly and took a long time to fill up. He was allowing himself to take in as much as he could and he let me know he was willing and open to the healing energy.

Then, I sent the healing to my 7-year-old daughter. She immediately took it in and was so joyful and full of bliss! She danced in the healing white light. I saw angel wings on her back as I did on my son Chad's back. She danced like a ballerina and soaked in the light. She was so joyful!

Lastly, I sent the light to my husband, who at first was not sure, but soon became open and receptive to the healing white light of Creator's love. As soon as he accepted the light, a dark shadow in front of him melted and a white dove flew out of his back (representing peace and love). He stood up and gave me so much love and hugged me! The whole room lit up with white light! It was amazing to feel so much love between my husband and I. It was such a powerful experience!

In my Sacred Space – My 3rd Vision

As I sat on my couch, I felt a hand gently wrap around my left arm. I knew it was my grandmother letting me know it was her turn to visit me. I put my hand on top of hers and let her know I love her and miss her.

When I went to the sacred place, I saw green grass and a bright light heading towards me. The light came in front of me and I asked who it was, it was my grandmother! She said she loved me and that everything was going to be alright. She went on to tell me to continue to give lots of love and share the feeling of love with those around me. She told me to no longer worry about her death, "I died in peace." she had died in my arms. She asked me to forgive someone I was angry with over the years. I was so happy to see her and was relieved to hear her say she died in peace. For years I worried about her death, wondering if I caused her death. I wondered if she was sick with something and somehow, I missed it because she was in my care. I thanked her for the message and for all the love she shared with me and for her teachings. I asked her if she wanted to join me on my journey and she said yes.

We walked together down my sacred path to find a gate with my sacred symbol on it. I opened the door and both of us walked in. I saw myself inside a home where my grandparents took me as a baby at a summer camp called Northeast Cape. A mountain called my attention and I asked why it had come to me, "Fight for your people by sending a positive message to the military, asking them to please come back for what they left. We are all people and we should work together in peace and harmony". The mountain thanked me for what I will be doing for Mother Earth and our people. I thanked the mountain for the message and said I would do what was asked of me, knowing that spirit and your ancestors would guide me, using me as a vehicle of God's good work. The U.S. Military had left a chemical waste site from WWII that leaked into our lands and waters and caused our people cancer over the years. The military never returned to clean up the waste site. Our people have been battling against the military to clean up what they left behind. As a result of this waste site, the people of St. Lawrence Island have one of the highest rates of cancer.

I found my sacred water nearby and there I found a cup. I noticed it changed a little from a Styrofoam cup to a glass cup. I dipped it into the sacred water and drank nearly a full cup and it felt so pure going down my throat that I could hardly feel it. I went into the sacred water to soak myself to remove negative energies. I saw a dark ink like energy being released from my mind, body, and spirit. Once the ink cleared, I got out of the water and looked at my reflection on the water's edge. I saw the woman again, who was no longer in her 90s, but appeared to be in her 60s, looking at me with dark brown, shining, smiling eyes. Her aura was green (healer's energy). She told me a message, "Work with people of all Nations. You have a powerful gift, so use it. Touch people and pray for them with your healing hands." I asked when I should start using my gift outside my family and friends. She told me that I would know when the time was right. "We are happy you are doing this work." I thanked Creator and my ancestors for all they are doing on my behalf and the gifts I have received to help people. I asked her once again, since I had seen her in my previous visions who she was, "I carry you, you carry me." I suddenly realized she was my great-grandma Yaari. It was her and she said, "You often wondered what kind of person I was, you're just like me."

As I continued back to my sacred path, I came to a nenglu (sod house). There in the center of the house, I found a bright light. I picked up the bright light and it said it wanted to live in me, so I asked where in my body, "In your head." The light would eliminate the fog in my head so I could see more clearly. As it moved inside my head, I felt clarity like I had never experienced before. Chills moved throughout my entire body!

In my Sacred Space – My 4th Vision

I see the sun, very clear and beautiful! I found my grandmother on my mother's side there waiting for me. I asked why she came forward. She said she loved me and watched over me. I let her know I loved her too and missed her. She asked me to bring the family together as I have become distant over the years. She asked me to have them over for dinner to bring them closer together. I asked her if she had any other messages. She said my grandfather, that was in a wheelchair, wanted to thank me for taking care of him and for being there for him. Tears rolled down my cheeks. She wanted me to connect with my Uncle Perry and to stay in touch with him for he was lonely for his parents. She went on to tell me to show more love for my mother. I asked my grandmother why my mother was distant from my siblings and me. She said it had to do with her being adopted. She felt abandoned by her birth parents and that affected her presently. My grandmother asked me to speak to my mother and let her know she was loved very much and is still loved. I promised my grandmother I would speak to my mother and become close to her and Uncle Perry.

I went to my sacred water, where I noticed my glass had changed into a golden goblet. I drank one full cup of the sacred water that felt as if my ancestors were singing through me. I don't know quite how to explain it. I felt so much inner peace and purity! I got in the sacred water to heal as I had been through so much the last week. I could see the dark ink-like energy leaving my mind, body, and spirit.

I went into a nenglu (sod house) and there in the center of the room were women dressed in traditional white clothes. They told me they were all mothers and were here to help remind me how important children are, "You need to communicate to your children and help them to embrace who they are and where they come from. Teach your children more of the traditional values and dances, and take them home so they can experience our culture. This will connect them with the land so that they have respect for Mother Earth and what she provides for them." The women ended by saying they were so proud of me and to continue teaching our values.

Back on my sacred path, I came to the fish camp called Alngighyak where our family fished each summer. I was taken there because I loved it there so much growing up. My ancestors wanted my children and husband to experience what I did at fish camp.

Just as I was heading back to my sacred path, an energy of white light approached me and I asked who it was, my grandfather on my mother's side! Oh! How happy I was! He wanted to thank me for taking care of him when he needed me the most. He was very grateful for the love and devotion I showed him. He went on to say to take care of my body that the spirit world was asking me to do so. I asked my grandfather how I should take care of myself better, he said to actively, physically walk and dance more. He went on to say to love my mom and that she needed me, "You need to let her know she was not rejected, she was loved very much. She is a gift from Creator." I let him know I would share with her. I asked him if he had any more messages, "Yes. Do not carry so much stress from other people. That is why your shoulder hurts you. Take care of yourself". I said my I love you to him and he went down the path.

In my Sacred Space – My 5th Vision

I found myself on the tundra on a path that used to be of our ancestors. It was walked on so much that it was packed down hard into the ground. I saw our ancestors alongside the path, drumming, clapping, and singing with joy. They were so happy for me! All at once, I saw so much green aura light around me and I asked my ancestors what it was for, "For healing people, but first you must heal yourself, then help others. You will connect with God and through prayer he will guide you to do the work you need to do for others. You will also use your healing hands to help others and you will be guided through Creator in prayer, he will reveal what you need to do. We are proud of you. Never be afraid, when Creator is with you, no one can be against you. You are a vehicle for Creator's work and he will work through you as he helps his people. Creator is leading the way. Your shoulder is hurting because you are taking on the worries, burdens, and pain of people that you are helping. You are not to take on people's pains, and you are to turn it over to Creator so he can heal them." I was told to call upon the shield of Creator to protect myself from harm.

I then saw a deep, blue-colored light come to me, the same color as my third eye. The light told me it came to help open my 3rd eye so that I can see better, and be connected to the spirit world. My ancestors will be working with me and they were happy that they could help me. As a result, I felt my spine get stronger. I learned that in the ancient way of looking at things, our spine represents our ancestors. I felt so much strength and love knowing I am an instrument of Creator's work and what an honor that is! I also received a yellow, bright light as a gift.

As I went on my sacred path, I saw another bright light and I asked who it was, it was my two youngest children's grandfather. He told me to continue teaching my children and to let them know he loves them and that he is proud of them. He asked me to continue to pray for family and others and that I was doing the right thing. He thanked me for being accepting. He finished by saying he loved me. I let him know I love him too and I thanked him.

Message from my Ancestors

My ancestors came to me and told me that I needed to drum and sing more for it would soothe my spirit and soul. The drumming and singing will help me to connect with my ancestors who are here to help me. They went on to say, "Teach your children who they are, teach them their language and take them back home so they can connect with the land. Love yourself more and eat more traditional foods. People will bring you food and it will heal your body, mind, and spirit."

I then felt a push on my forehead and I asked the ancestors what it was. They said I was now promoted to the next level. I was about to experience more and grow more with my gifts. They told me I was going to become masterful with my spiritual gifts. I was told my ancestors and Creator would warn me when I begin to go on the wrong path, "Eat healthy foods and sing your songs." I saw so much green aura around me.

Creator Speaks to Me

"I want you to read the bible, for it is my truth and the way of life. You will learn the truth by reading the bible and you will learn how to protect yourself. I want you to study the bible."

In my Sacred Space – My 6th Vision

I saw water in front of me with blue skies above me and there was some fog that was present. The fog told me it was "Goodness from Creator", and that when I go places and see people, it would bring me peace and love. The fog energy would open up the heart for me to share Creator's love, peace, and forgiveness as I help others. The fog goes on to tell me that I would do it through hugging people to send them love into their bodies. The fog told me it would never be me, that it would be Creator using me as a tool. I asked the fog if I would be protected, "You must continue to practice what you were taught about protecting yourself as you have been taught by using the shield of Creator, smudging yourself and your home". "What else?" I asked the fog, "Keep doing what you're doing, you are on the right path. Speak to your children about Creator." I asked the fog how do I reach my son, "Read the Bible with him; speak heart to heart with him showing him that you love him. Send him Creator's love." I asked if there was anything else I needed to know, "Read the bible with your husband. He will teach you what you do not understand. He was raised with the bible and he will teach you."

At my sacred water, I found my sacred cup, it had changed once again. It was still the same golden goblet, but it was bigger. I dipped it into the sacred water and drank one full cup and it was sparkly and it filled me with light and love.

I went into the sacred water and I did not need much healing. My body was filled with Creator's healing light and love. When I came out of the water, I looked at my reflection and saw a 16-year-old girl looking at me. She was so happy and she told me that I had to move on from what happened to me at the age of 16 and that I should no longer carry the pain. She thanked me for my work and for releasing her from feeling trapped within me for so many years. She went on to say, "Finish writing your book. I will help you write and guide you through the writing. Pray before you write on the weekends when you are most at peace." I promised her I would write and it made me feel joy. I asked her if there were any more messages, "Yes. Listen to your son's heart and you will better understand him." I asked her where in my body she would like to live, "In your bones." I thanked her for the gift of words and for the writing that we would be doing together and also for healing.

I went on my path and noticed it was greener and brighter. On the path I came to a tree that gave me the energy of the gift of love. I asked how it would help me, "When you touch people with your pointer finger, you will send them positive energy, the gift of the Creator's love and light, which will bring them peace. I asked where in my body it would like to live, "In your shoulder." When the healing light entered my body, I could feel so much energy moving throughout my body filling me up with love and positive energy. I could feel how much love I had to offer that was all coming from Creator. I was told to begin healing my family and myself first then move on to helping others. I asked if there were any more messages, "Take care of yourself and your shoulder so that it may become stronger again, then you can begin to help the people."

In my Sacred Space – My 7th Vision

I found myself at a fish camp on St. Lawrence Island. The horizon and the ocean were so clear! Spirit said, "Come visit here with your children. They need to learn the value of cutting fish and putting it away. They need to learn where they come from and their ancestors will guide them." I asked what was the urgency of coming home, "There is work to be done here with your people."

At my sacred water, I saw a cup. It was white sparkling cup like sparkling snow energy. I drank a full cup of water that felt healing to the pain in my shoulder. When I went into the sacred water, I again received healing to my mind, body, and spirit with the understanding that I had taken on too much from other people. The sacred water took out all the negative energy from my mind, body, and spirit, allowing me to return to the bright light it once held. As I stepped out of the water, I saw a reflection from the water's edge. The reflection told me it was the 16-year-old me with a turquoise aura, which was the communicator. She told me to continue to do self-care.

Something amazing happened! Creator wanted me to do healing work on my friend and also with my Traditional Healer guide, Laura! The creator sent a message to her saying he was going to bless her and promote her to becoming a teacher of many students at once. I saw an angel touch her back to heal her. Her great-grandmother came forward, saying she was proud of Laura. I was able to see everything that was taking place in Laura's spiritual life and what Creator was about to do for her. Laura felt the warmth of her grandmother and Creator's love.

I then approached a tree where I received a turquoise energy that will give me the gift of the communicator (meaning being used by Creator to communicate with others). All I had to do was open my mouth and relax and Creator would speak through me, "The words that come out of your mouth would not be the words of yours, but the words of our Creator. These words will help with healing in people's lives. When the words flow out of your mouth do not be afraid. Continue to learn the bible and read it with your children and husband. When you read the bible, the gift Creator has given you will help you to understand the bible deeply." I asked the turquoise energy where in my body it wanted to live, "In your backbone. The energy will help you to stand up and I will help you to speak. When you speak, you will feel the power of the Creator coming through you. Sometimes, you will say that are harsh truths and it will not be easy for some to hear at first, but they will come to see it will help them. Continue to tell your husband the messages you are receiving from the Creator. Trust in the words that come out of your mouth, they are coming from Creator." The energy that Creator is giving you will strengthen you so that you will not take on the burdens of others. That is why the energy was placed at your backbone, it will strengthen you." Anything else? "A message for Laura: Each morning, get a cup of water and pray over it, asking Creator to fill it up with the healing white light of his love, drink it down and it will heal your body and wash away any unwanted energy from your body. Continue to cleanse yourself each day, say your mantra, pray to Creator, and continue to spread the light of God. You are on the right track."

In my Sacred Space – My 8th Vision

Creator wakes me in the middle of the night sometimes so I can pray for someone in need. I wake up and a headache begins on my left temple, sometimes a very bright light flickers on my left side. This I learned, is a sign for me to pray for someone or about something. The Creator woke me up to pray about the community of Anchorage and its homeless population. During prayer, he showed me a vision; I saw many indigenous people who woke and began to heal people. Creator told me that the healers would come from the North. I saw many Traditional Healers working with the homeless. Some homeless people received healing, got jobs, some started families, and some joined us to heal others. As healers worked with people, angels floated behind them.

In my Sacred Space – My 9th Vision

The Creator spoke to me and requested I begin to pray and meditate at work. I started doing that as soon as he requested. During prayer and meditation one morning, my grandfather, my grandmother, and the rest of the ancestors joined me in prayer in a circle in the Gathering Place. As we all prayed together, Creator showed me a vision. A small bright light formed in the heart of the Alaska Native Heritage Center. I asked Creator what it was, "The light represents growth and expansion. The indigenous people will begin to come forward to the Alaska Native Heritage Center for healing. The number of healers will grow and be utilized. Some staff will be skeptical, but will eventually come to believe. Some visitors from the outside will be curious and take part in healing with the indigenous people, but healing must start with the staff first." I asked the Creator if that was why he requested me to start praying and meditating at work, "Yes. We are cleaning it up together."

The Changes I Started to Notice

I began to notice some changes for the better in my life. I also started to experience the unseen or the unknown more often than usual. I had asked Creator to show me signs at his will and a song came to me,

"Blessed assurance Jesus is mine." I could feel Creator speaking to my heart. I felt such a strong sense of warmth and calmness. I began to see lights all around me as Creator told me they were angels to protect me. Creator spoke to my heart and told me to trust him, be patient, and allow things to happen in their own time and in his way. I felt so much more at peace. My memory was getting better. I also saw about 15-20 angels surrounding my house in my dream. I also learned when I pray, Creator shows me who to pray for and lets me know what to pray about. During some of my prayers Creator would give me a vision (prophecy).

In My Sacred Space – My Grandmother Mabel's Birthday
September 1, 2019

Grandma Mabel was dressed in all white. She looked young and beautiful with her hair braided with qupaks (beads). She put three white marks on my forehead going down. She said, "Self-discipline your mind, body, and spirit. Practice what you preach." I thanked my grandmother for reminding me. I then asked God to guide me and remind me to practice what my grandmother reminded me of. Then my dad and Apa came forward with one eagle feather each. They put them over my arms with the tip of the feather over my fingers. I asked what they were for, they said when I use my hands to brush people off and to imagine these eagle feathers on my hands and brush people's negative energies off. I saw a river so I jumped in to cleanse my being. I saw trees on each side. Creator urged me to spread the water of the river over the trees to protect them and to allow it to rain over the forest fires to put them out. I was urged by Creator to drink 3 cups of riiglluk (stinkweed) tea daily and he said I'll know when to stop. I thanked Creator for my ancestors and for coming to be with me. I returned from my journey and brushed myself off with my hands, imagining the eagle feathers on each side of my arms and hands. Creator also wanted me to do healing sessions with the men who are helping us with our triplex. A time will be revealed to me and open a way for us.

Chapter Sixteen

The Last Time

    My father and my brother came into town for my father's heart appointments. They were in town for a couple of days. His ticker was in good condition so he got the okay from his doctor to go home. The next morning the cab came to take them to the airport. I walked them out the door, hugged them and said our I love yous and sent them off in their cab. As I turned around to go back into the house, I knew right away that it was going to be the last time I would ever speak to my dad. I paused when I felt it, but made myself believe it wasn't true. They left in the cab and that was it. Two days later, I got a call saying my father was in a bad four-wheeler accident 80 miles out of the village. There was no way to get him immediate help. Someone at home contacted the Alaska Coast Guard for help. They picked my father up in a helicopter and flew him to Nome. My father was then sent to Anchorage on an emergency.

    The plane finally arrived. I was too scared to see my father's condition, so I hesitated to go see him at ER. I had to be brave to go be with him so I went. He had a very bad head injury. He was partially sedated so he would not suffer. When I finally saw him, I held his hand. I said to my dad, "Dad if you can hear me, squeeze my hand three times if you want Mom to come be with you." he squeezed my hand three times. I spoke to his doctor and he said it was really bad. There was no way to tell just yet if my dad was going to be okay or not. He was kept sedated in the Intensive Care Unit. My mother and my siblings flew to Anchorage to be with our dad. It was hard to watch my dad suffer at the hospital for two weeks. Things got worse for him. He had a major stroke. The doctor had a meeting with our family. The news was not good. He told our family that our father would always be in a vegetable state because he had no brain activity. My dad was basically brain-dead. The only thing that kept him alive was the life support machine. I requested another opinion from another doctor and by another doctor. They both told us the same thing the first doctor did. We were all devastated by the news. It was not good.

I called my uncles to tell them the news. I asked them what we should do. My uncles told me it was up to me because I was the oldest child. I spoke to my mother out of respect to get her input, but my mother said it was up to me. I asked my siblings, and they told me the same thing. I prayed and I cried, I prayed and I cried. I told my siblings I wanted to keep him on life support. My sister said, "This is not living. Dad would not want to suffer like this." My sister was right. I told my family that we were going to spend the last two days with him before we took him off life support. The day before we unplugged the machine, we asked people in the community to come help our family celebrate my father's life by "Eskimo" dancing with us. People came to the hospital lobby and danced with us. I announced to the people that we decided to let go of our dad. Everyone was quiet, some people in tears.

The next day, we spent our last morning with him. My uncle and aunt drove from Fairbanks to be with us. My mother kept leaving the room. I could feel her anxiety. Our father hung onto life for four hours without life support. He hung on until our mother came to hold his hand. I told my dad it was okay to let go. He opened his eyes and looked into mine as if he were telling me we would be okay. He took his last breath. I suddenly felt like I was an orphaned child, even if I was a grown adult. My dad! My heart was heavy. We all prayed and cried together. It was one of the most painful emotions I had ever felt.

Our father was our emotional support, giving us structure and treating us with love and respect. When my father passed away in 2017, I asked my husband what he and my father talked about. He wasn't supposed to tell me, but he decided to tell me. My husband said, "Your father told me everything about the abuse. He made me promise him that I would take good care of his baby girl. I am going to keep my promise to him and to you." I know my dad sees. He knows that he takes good care of us and protects us.

My husband and I flew home to lay my father to rest. It was his first time ever in a Rural Alaskan village. After my father's funeral, the men in my village asked me how our family wanted to bring him to his final resting place: by pulling a wagon with him in it by foot or four-wheeler. I requested they pull him in the wagon on foot. About 20 men walked, pulling the wagon with my dad. It was heartbreaking to see my father being taken to his grave, but at the same time it was a beautiful sight to see that people cared and respected him. While we were at home at my mother's, I saw how young boys and men respected my parents. Young men came by my mother's house and asked her if she needed help with anything or if she needed anything. One day we came home to my mother's and she was crying. I asked if she was okay. She said someone gifted her a whole reindeer carcass and she didn't even know who it was. It was an anonymous person. Young men fixed my mother's windows and her steps outside. They brought her chopped firewood, bought her heating fuel, and delivered it to her house. I was in awe to see how much they respected and cared for my mother. I knew it also had to do with how my father was in the community. He volunteered countless hours to help people build their homes. He helped fix stuff at people's homes and never charged them for it. He shared food with other families when he hunted and fished. He took care of the people in the village. I wanted to be just like my father. I remember one day, I told my father that I wanted to be like his father, my grandfather. He said, "Look at yourself in the mirror, you are already just like him.". My grandfather was a true leader in the community who loved his people so much. He was highly respected in the community when he was alive. He was very wise, patient, and positive. He and my grandmother, who helped raise me, gave me a lot of structure and wisdom. My grandfather taught me about what a leader is in our culture and my grandmother was Yupik strict. She instilled good behavior in us using our St. Lawrence Island traditional values. Thanks to both of them I live my life with the values of our people that were passed down through generations by our ancestors. Although I sometimes make human mistakes and poor choices, I am reminded of how to be. I try my best to correct myself and ask for forgiveness.

Grieving for my father was very tough on me. My heart was heavy daily. My siblings and I would call each other and cry together. Every time I called my mom, she would be crying. My mother had asked my father the day before he passed away, "Dad, with your permission, I would like to stay a while longer so I could watch our grandchildren." That made all of us cry. I was very hurt for my mother. They were married for nearly 50 years. I remember my mom telling us children the story of how our dad waited for her. When my mother was sent to a boarding school, she told my dad he didn't have to wait for her to return and that he could date other girls if he wanted to. My dad did not want that, so he waited for my mom to graduate from high school. They had been together since.

Chapter Seventeen

Healing Center

I started to want a healing center in the community for all walks of life. I knew everyone needed healing, not just our Alaska Native people. One day, while I was at work, I overheard my co-workers talking about college. Something in my head said, "Apply for college" At that very moment, I got on my computer to attend Alaska Pacific University in Anchorage, majoring in Counseling Psychology with a Bachelor of Arts. Several weeks later I heard from APU saying I was accepted. I cried happy tears! I spoke to my father out loud, "Dad! I am finally going to college, something you've always wanted me to do! I will do this for you and the community to help bring healing!" I studied counseling psychology without a minor. I brought a wealth of Alaska Native knowledge to the university. I took school very seriously, knowing that I would someday work with people in the community. I really enjoyed my classes and I loved to write. I enjoyed researching and learning. For my senior year project, I decided to write about my culture, but I asked myself where I would find 15-20 peer-reviewed sources. I was only able to find three sources close to my topic. I didn't know where to find the rest of the sources. I decided to write from my heart and the knowledge passed down to me, especially my paternal grandparents. At the end of my 20+ page paper, I wrote, "Everything I shared with you was already peer-reviewed by my ancestors." I was afraid I would receive an "F" for a grade. I told my husband that the university would either take what I wrote and do something with it, or I was going to receive an F. My grade from that paper came back an "A+" WOW! I was so surprised and extremely happy!

I graduated from APU, majoring in Counseling Psychology, with a Bachelor of Arts degree in May of 2021. After I graduated, I sat down and thought about my journey in life. I went from being abused as a child by my mother, being violated by two adult men, experiencing domestic violence for 10+ years, alcoholism, homelessness, serving time at Hiland Mountain Correctional Center, going to treatment more than once, becoming sober, going to college and obtaining my degree, to now working with people in recovery from addiction from substance misuse. I enjoy using Alaska Native cultures and traditions and turning them into a curriculum with a focus on healing and growth at my job. I finally felt like I was doing my heart's work.

My dream is to help Alaska open a healing center with others in the community who are like-minded. Not to shame behavioral health programs, treatment centers and homeless shelters, but to me, these are band-aids. They give you great tools and resources to use in the community, but they do not go to the source of the pain or problem. I once had a 16-year-old girl who was trapped inside me. She stayed inside me until she was set free through Traditional Healing after 30+ years. Our spirits need healing too, not just our mental being.

I believe if professionals and healers worked together, we would make much progress with healing. We need both professionals and healers. I believe there would be more understanding of historical trauma. I believe people would be healthier emotionally, mentally, physically, and spiritually. When the system incorporates our holistic ways, we will have healers in every place where people receive services. I believe that someday it will happen. Maybe not in my lifetime, but someday.

Forgiveness

I started to think more and more about forgiveness in general. I no longer wanted to carry anger and resentment. I wanted to live more at peace. I worked towards forgiving my mother and my first husband, but now I needed to forgive the two men who violated my body. I want to be set free from anger, pain, and resentment. Even if I did not tell the two men I forgave them verbally, I would still forgive them through God. I have love for all in my heart, but I cannot love properly without forgiveness. It's time to move on and forgive.

Chapter Eighteen

Triggers

I went to Iceland in November of 2022 to act in True Detective Season 4 for HBO and spent four weeks in Reykjavik. I remember everywhere I went, there was alcohol. I walked into a building, and there it was. It triggered me and it made me feel so anxious and uncomfortable. I didn't want to leave my hotel room, so I hid for a couple of days. It wasn't that I was tempted to drink. It just reminded me of what an ugly person I was under the influence of alcohol. I felt so very ugly on the inside! I cried a lot. I felt like I hated myself all over again. It made me feel very sick to my stomach. I looked in the mirror and told myself out loud, "You are no longer this drunk person. You are sober. You are in a healthy relationship. You are strong. You graduated from college, and now you help others." It helped me a huge deal to do that and I felt better after that. I decided that I was not going to let alcohol take power over me, but I took power over it. I no longer felt triggered by it once I claimed my power. I no longer was triggered when I went to places where alcohol was served. I felt stronger on the inside and it made me feel good.

Chapter Nineteen

I'm a Survivor

I'm a survivor of child abuse and domestic violence. Beat with a broomstick, hit, and kicked by my mother. Broken bones, countless bruises, and my personal belongings being torn or broken by my first husband. I'm a survivor of my body being violated by two grown men. I'm a survivor of alcoholism, homelessness, and serving time at Hiland Mountain Correctional Center. I lived a very dysfunctional lifestyle in my addiction. I'm a survivor of asphyxiation, huffing gasoline and shoe goop. I could have died 10,000 times over. I am resilient. I am strong. I am worthy. I am loved. I am made up of DNA by my ancestors who come from different parts of the world. I exist because of them and, most of all Creator. I am who I am today because of the past and the now. I am in no way perfect and I am no better than anyone, but better than what I was. I'm in competition only with myself. Remember, this writing isn't only about me, it is about people who cannot voice for themselves. I'm a voice of thousands of people. I'm making good trouble.

Every single one of us has gone through hardships in our lives. Our stories may have some similarities but we've also had different traumatic events that happened to each of us. We all have trials and tribulations that could potentially make us stronger if we put our mindset into it. We just have to make up our minds. Regardless of your ethnicity, preferences, backgrounds, fight with me for your life and mine. Be an ally for all people.

Conclusion

In conclusion, I want to end it with an apology for anyone I may have hurt along my journey. They say hurt people, hurt people. I cannot take back the hurt and pain I may have caused, whether intentionally or unintentionally. I hope you can forgive me, whether by your heart or in person. I also forgive those who have hurt me in my past. My thoughts and words for you are to lift you up using love and prayers. Piniiqelleq atuqluku – Use love, and so I shall. Sometimes I forget and I need to be reminded too. I'm very grateful to everyone who crossed my path because I have learned much from others. No way am I shaming anyone because it is not in my heart. I hope you each have received the healing you need because everyone deserves healing. I wrote to give hope and understanding.

As my friend once asked, "Who did you write the book for?" I wrote it for the homeless man who stands at the corner of Northern Lights and C Street. I wrote it for a professor who teaches at a university. I wrote it for the therapists and counselors so they could better understand about relationships the Alaska Native way. I wrote it for the child who fears their parent. I wrote it for the abused and the abuser because they both need healing. I wrote it for youth so they know to get help when it is needed instead of using negative coping skills. I wrote it for middle school and high school students for life skills. I wrote it for people who work in recovery services and for those who are in recovery services. I wrote this for our parents, grandparents, and great-grandparents who endured abuse while in residential schools. What happened to you was not your fault. I wrote it for the reader because we all need healing.

For My Mother

  I learned this story from a friend many years ago. How our drum came to be, "Ungipaghaaninguq imaani, a long time ago, a mother Eagle came to our people and told us we needed to make drums to honor our mothers. The mother Eagle showed our people what kind of material to use to make our drums. The drum frame is made out of driftwood, carved into a thin strip, and then steam-bent into a round shape. The drum handle is made out of either walrus ivory or bone. The covering of the drum is made out of the inner lining of a walrus's stomach. A groove would be carved around the drum to hold the drum covering and frame together using sinew ligaments from large animals. The drumstick is made out of baleen, which comes from the mouth of the bowhead whale. The mother Eagle started to beat the drum from the backside and told our people that the beat of the drum represented our mother's heartbeat. So, in honor of our mothers, we have our drums to this day. Today, I also use my drum for healing as my ancestors told me, "Keep singing your songs, stay healthy and strong." Mom, I will always think of you when I drum and sing. The beat of my drum is a reminder to honor and love you.

  Mom, I wrote this for my brother, sister, you and I because we all need healing. You are loved, you are special, you are a jewel, a gift from above. I forgave you a million times over and over. Whatever happened to you while in residential school was not your fault. I'm so very sorry for whatever you may have endured. I was I was there to protect you. You forever have a very special place in my heart. I love you, mom.

Acknowledgements

I would like to acknowledge and thank my friends Cindy Calzada, Carly Richey, and Travis Shinabarger who sat with me for five and a half hours listening to me read my writing and helped me with grammar and punctuation. Thank you each for your patience, support and the respect you showed me while you listened to me read to you.

To my former supervisors from the Alaska Native Heritage Center, thank you for believing in me and for giving me a chance to grow. You've helped me grow so much and even helped me to learn more about myself. Thank you for pushing me to get the help I needed with my addiction. You will forever be in my heart!

To my best friends Joy and Tiffany, I could never thank you both enough for always being there for me, even if it was difficult in my intoxication. You made sure I was safe. You protected me even if I may have been mad at you for silly reasons, you stood by my side. How did I get so lucky to have you both?! I love you both endlessly!

To my children, I'm sorry for all I've put you through and I'm sorry you had to see me in my addiction. I can only hope that you can forgive me. I cannot take back all the pain I've caused you, but I will be here for you for the rest of my days and I will always love you forever. I'm sorry I was not the mom you needed me to be, but here I am.

To my husband, you never gave up on me, even after we split as boyfriend and girlfriend. You stood by my side and walked with me. You allowed me to scream and cry while you held me. You comforted me and told me I would be okay even. Your words helped me to feel better because some moments I thought I would never be okay again. Thank you for helping me through my hardest and darkest times. My love for you only grows deeper and deeper daily. You are stuck with me (I can see us LOL together)!

To my late grandparents, I will never forget the moments I've had with you and all the love you shared with me, the things you taught me through stories and your words. Apa Donald, thank you for allowing me to help take care of you. I loved caring for you when you lived with us at Mom and Dad's. I always wanted to be there for you. Grandma Laura, I remember you always used to tell me "The Toolie's stole you from us." I never knew exactly what you meant by that until I asked Mom one day. Mom married Dad when she was pregnant with me. I still belong to you too. Apa Tulii, the man who taught me how to be a leader using our traditional values, reminded me daily how to be, and encouraged me to work through trials and tribulations. Grandma Mabel, a strict woman you were. I needed that. You taught me about attitude and behavior. Forever I am grateful for each of you. All of you have helped shape me into who I am today. Some day, I will dance with you in heaven.

Mom and Dad, thank you for bringing me into this world. Dad, thank you for giving us structure and being strict with us. I now understand what you meant when you used to tell me, "I know nothing. Talk to my older brothers." And when I asked you why I should go to them, you used to tell me, "Because they have more experience than I do and they are wiser." I tell people the same today, "I know nothing." Mom, thank you for loving me and thank you for the apology. I forgave you many years ago. My mama forever!

Late paternal grandmother Mabel Legraaghaq Toolie (left) and late paternal grandfather Jimmie Tulii Toolie (right).

My paternal late grandfather Jimmie Tulii Toolie.

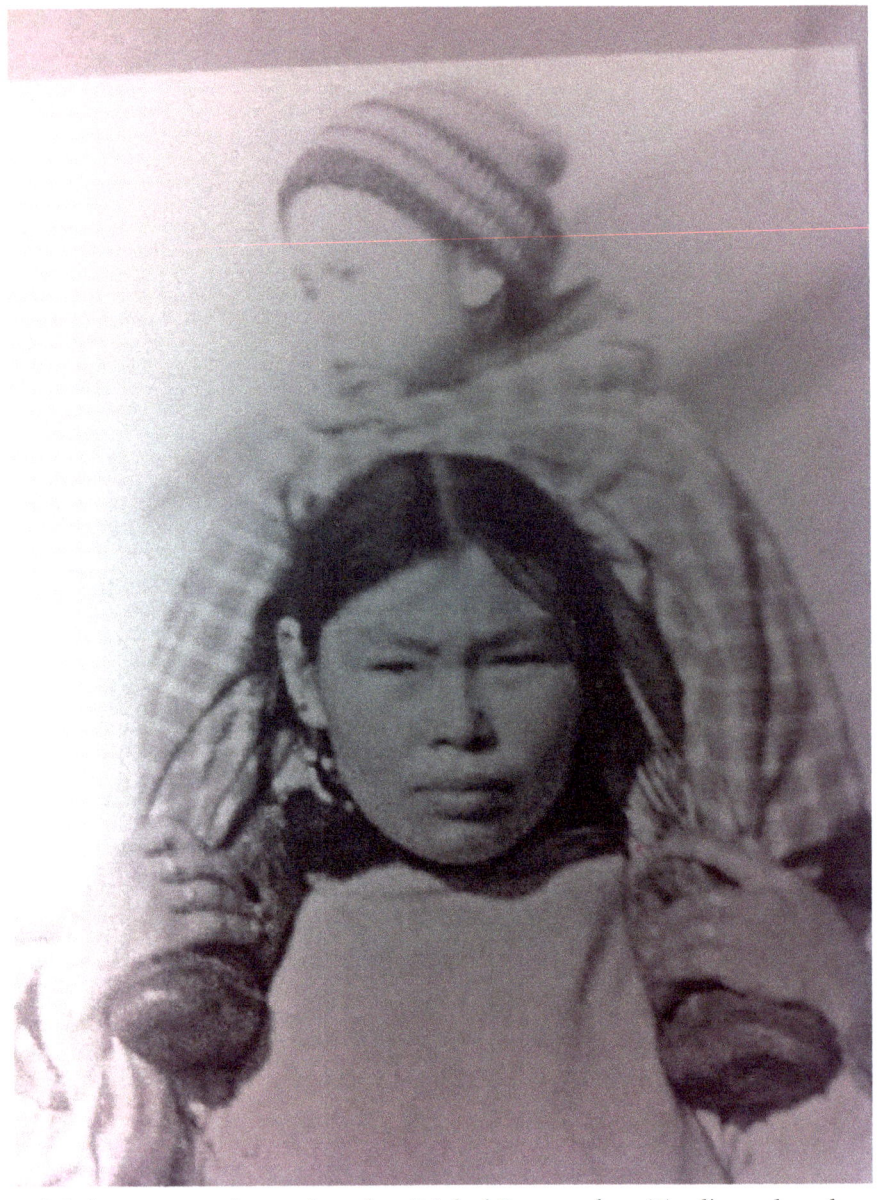

My late paternal grandmother Mabel Legraaghaq Toolie and on her shoulders her oldest late daughter Katherine Qunglliin Noongwook

My late maternal grandmother Laura Ikaanuq Pungowiyi.

Herman Pegetkaq Toolie (late father).

My late father Herman, mother Esther Toolie and mother-in-law
And father-in-law, Carlene and Larry Walker.

Allyssa Asicksik

My oldest daughter Laura Toolie (left) and my second son, Daryl Kingeekuk

My sons Theo Kingeekuk (far left), Chad Kingeekuk (top) and Daryl Kingeekuk (bottom).

My oldest son Miller Kingeekuk

God, thank you for the life that you gave me. Thank you for my trials and tribulations; they helped me grow and strengthen. Thank you for paving the way for me and for guiding me. Thank you for spirituality and for healing. My love for you is indescribable! I just know I love you BIGGEST! I will serve you and the people.

Love, Yaari

About the Author

Yaari Walker wrote about her personal experience of child abuse, sexual assault, domestic violence, alcoholism, serving at a correctional center, going to treatment and her healing journey. She used substance treatment for her healing journey and used substances like alcohol as a coping mechanism.

She wrote about her personal experiences with cultural sensitivity and inter-ethnic communication because of the cultural differences.

"'Keep paddling against the wind.' By Jimmie Toolie." Yaari's apa (grandfather) often told her this to encourage her to work through challenges and obstacles.

www.ingramcontent.com/pod-product-compliance
Lightning Source LLC
Chambersburg PA
CBHW041146110526
44590CB00027B/4144